"Debi is the epitome of achievable perfection—she's like the Martha Stewart next door! Her simple yet extraordinary ideas are things anyone can do. I had the pleasure of working with Debi for more than 10 years on Oprah. From the big red bows in the You Get a Car! Giveaway Show to the perfectly wrapped gifts on "Oprah's Favorite Things...," I wouldn't produce a big show without Debi—our very own Mary Poppins, practically perfect in every way, producing mind-blowing events you'll never forget."

—Gina Sprehe, EXECUTIVE PRODUCER, OPRAH WINFREY NETWORK

"Debi Lilly is Chicago's own and one of America's most talented party designers and planners. She has created the most magical, memorable events for my celebrity clients—from Chicago to LA. Love is in the details—well, it's more than love for Debi—it's pure passion."

—Art Smith, CELEBRITY CHEF AND AUTHOR

"Debi and her team of magicians bring surprising, memorable moments to every event, from showers and weddings to birthdays and corporate events. From Oprah to that special four-year-old in your life, *A Perfect Event* delivers and innovates to bring to life those moments you'll never forget."

—Amy Cheronis, EVP, LEO BURNETT

"We have worked with Debi Lilly and "A Perfect Event" on many different event partnerships. Her level of professionalism, passion, expertise, creativity, and tremendous talent produces the most fantastic results transforming the ordinary into extraordinary. There is no mistaking the Debi Lilly magic touch."

— Mimi Clark, BLOOMINGDALES

"For several years, Debi has designed our parties and events, and my expectations are consistently exceeded. I have never worked with a more talented, more dedicated, and more creative team than Debi and the "A Perfect Event" staff. She is amazing, and our go-to expert!"

— Peggy Lanigan, MOËT & CHANDON

"Debi Lilly's effortless understanding of style and elegance affords her clients complete confidence in the final product she will help them achieve. Creativity, beauty, and ingenuity abound with all Debi touches. She is a true gem!"

— Kimberly Burt, DOM PERIGNON

"Debi Lilly always brings a great amount of energy and creativity to every single event. Debi has the passion that excites the client and the event industry professionals."

—Amanda Belton, THE RITZ CARLTON

"Whether an intimate gathering or large gala for hundreds Debi and her team make your event your own Perfect Event. As a hostess you can be confident your party will go off without a hitch and as a guest it will be the party you'll be talking about for years to come."

—Andrea Rich, AMERICAN HEART ASSOCIATION

Ladies tea party

a Perfect Event

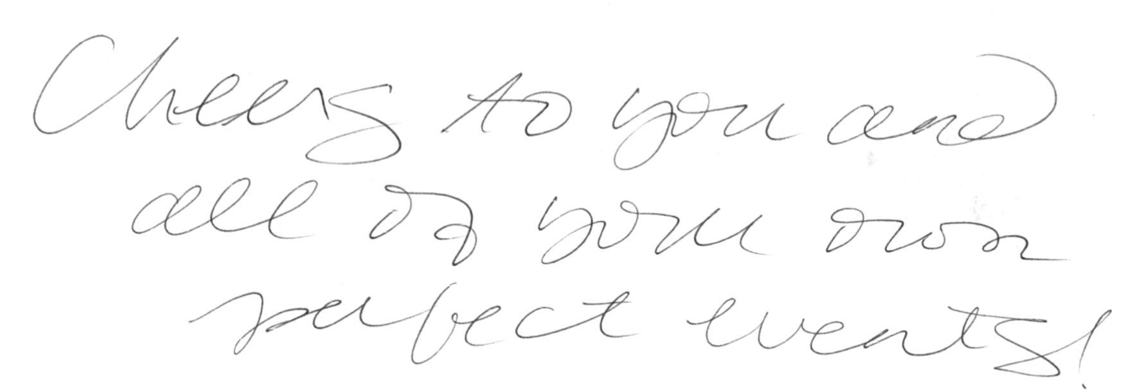

Menu
Debi
Cucumber with Cream Cheese

a Perfect Event

INSPIRED, EASY ELEGANCE FOR EVERY OCCASION

Grocery-to-Gorgeous Recipes,
Stylist Secrets, Affordable DIYs

Debi Lilly

DUNHAM
books

Dunham Books
63 Music Square East
Nashville, Tennessee 37203
www.dunhamgroupinc.com

Edited by Alice Sullivan
Designed by
Mary Sue Englund (Blu Design Concepts)
and Christa Schoenbrodt (Studio Haus)

Trade Paperback ISBN: 978-0-9851359-6-6
Ebook ISBN: 978-0-9851359-7-3

Printed in the United States of America

Contents

TO THE LADIES who have made my life so beautiful: Gigi—my grandmother Caroline Adams; my mother, the original Debbie Lilly; and my darling daughter, Lilly Caroline—three beloved generations of immense inspiration, creative talent, artistic teaching, crafty genius, and hearts as big as the universe. There aren't words to describe what you mean to me.

I AM BLESSED to have the same unbounded love and artistry from the boys in my life: my father Ron Lilly, whose renaissance talent knows no limit; my husband Mike Springer, who lovingly illustrated my vision for every party in these pages, and moves sun, moon, and stars to support our family and "A Perfect Event" on a daily—no—hourly basis; and my charming, sweet boy, Parker, who defies description.

INTRODUCTION

TO PEN A BOOK has been my lifelong dream. Seriously—my entire life long.

I started writing books when I was in second grade and even went to state for creative writing in Mrs. Carlson's class. This is such a crazy blessing to have you reading these words, on a printed page, in this glossy book.

Likewise, I have always loved a good party.

My mother, and my grandmother alike, made every family holiday and special occasion simply beautiful. Personal. Thoughtful. Family traditions were shared and celebrated.

When it came time for little school parties—I was up and at 'em, party dress pressed and ready, front and center of the line, ready to celebrate.

In fact, my earliest party memories are still as clear as a bell. My first wedding party occurred when I was all of five and I remember shopping for a fancy mint green–collared dress with my mom, and "helping" (doubtful) open all of the pretty wedding presents covering the floor of my grandparents' living room.

Then there was my great-grandparents' fiftieth anniversary party in our family kitchen. I sat at the table fascinated with the handmade "money tree" crafted just for the occasion.

I remember a kindergarten party at Emerson Elementary, at the tender age of five and a half. It was in celebration of a favorite book, called *Stone Soup*. We clever classmates scoured the schoolyard for the perfect, round, shiny stone—the *pièce de résistance* ingredient. We then ran—bursting through the door—into the classroom, and with freshly washed hands we chopped, diced, and prepared Stone Soup together as mini chefs.

Next, it simmered for what seemed like countless hours on end. This was during the course of our daily afternoon naptime schedule, which, of course, I absolutely did not understand. Who on earth could nap when we were party planning for Pete's sake? (Apparently even as a toddler, much to my mother's chagrin, I was much too busy for napping.)

When it was ready, soup was ladled into small paper cups for each student. We all watched with huge eyes as the teacher filled our cups—fingers crossed in anticipation that we would be holding the cup with the shiny stone in our soup.

I have absolutely no idea who "won" the stone that day. It don't recall any details, above and beyond all the planning and excitement. And that very day, I resolved that I needed to plan another party.

And I did. There were elaborate Christmas Cookie Decorating parties with all my girlfriends, Holiday Craft Bazaars with handmade ornaments (I was a crazy cross-stitcher thanks to my darling Grandmother), and gourmet gifts I baked from scratch. My neighbor Nancy didn't come to one very special bazaar, and just a few years ago, some thirty years later, she reminded me that I didn't speak to her for weeks.

I remember standing at my kitchen island as a young girl, pretending I was Julia Child, cooking and baking, whilst narrating each step (to no one but the refrigerator) in my make-believe kitchen "set."

My Girl Scout badges were all devised around crafting, cooking, and entertaining. I was enrolled in cooking and calligraphy classes while my friends took gymnastics, cheerleading, and dance. The youngest student by a mile, I was surrounded by forty and fifty somethings.

Two of my favorite memories are helping cater one of my dad's corporate parties in a super fancy, very official office building (wearing all black with a little white apron was such a thrill) and being large and in charge of my mom's surprise thirtieth birthday party. At least, that's what I thought.

In junior high school, you didn't take a vacation without me throwing you a "bon voyage" party. Or move into a new house without a proper "housewarming" party. My high school friends love to remind me that I celebrated all of the band members of Duran Duran's birthdays, complete with a full buffet serving each of their favorite foods. Sheesh.

In college, clearly I ran for etiquette chair my freshman year, followed by social chairman thereafter. I was also squeezing in catering alongside two fabulous French chefs, both having moved stateside from Paris, for years on end, whenever I had even a moment to spare.

By my senior year in college, I was helping my older friends with their weddings, catering small parties, and ready to burst for getting to the business of party planning full time. I launched A Perfect Event the very day after I graduated, and haven't looked back.

Fast forward to one thousand plus parties and twenty years later, I love nothing more than to inspire people to celebrate. From friends to family to my darling children—and even complete strangers, we just do not have, nor take the time to, celebrate each other enough. We are too busy, too stressed, life is too hectic, and we are too overscheduled. We are dual-income working families traveling each week, running our kids hither, thither, and yon. Who has time to invite the neighbors over for dinner?

Well, I have news for you. You can do it. Easily. Elegantly. Affordably. You have the time. Make the time. And I am going to show you how. Read on—inside our little black book of stylist secrets—how to make grocery goods into gorgeous, delicious décor and revered recipes. Turn off the TV, the iPad, and the computer games. Gather the kids around the kitchen table and create something together. Make memories. Build family traditions. What we do now with our children teaches the behavior they will model with their own future families. Let's make it all count—and let's have fun together while we do so.

Life is short. Life *is* the small moments. I have lost friends. I have lost family. We all have. I would give anything for one more afternoon spent together. So would you. So let's do it—together. Let's vow to stop, to celebrate, and to make the time for the small moments and for reflection of life's cherished memories.

Here we go.

chapter one

COCKTAILS, PLEASE

A COCKTAIL PARTY is the easy "go to" celebration: all the full-on fun, but with half the amount of work.

It's all about celebrating with friends and family for the ultimate get-together, generally done with a light bites menu. Throwing a cocktail party means less preparation and often less expense. And, yet, these simple, easy parties are usually the most memorable. Maybe it's because the host enjoys the party just as much as the gracious guests. Or, perhaps it's the high-energy, spirited conversation and merry mixing and mingling that makes for a party to remember.

Whatever the reason, a cocktail party is *always* in season. Creating a dramatic, memorable atmosphere makes a cocktail party the ultimate social gathering. An interesting drink or two is your fabulous focal point. All you need are a few simple details to complete the event: a light, interesting menu, some great music, and an inviting party palate. Cheers to the classic, old-school cocktail party! Now... ready to come inside?

In this chapter you'll find:

- *Cocktails with Art & Giada*
- *Winter Wonderland*
- *Spa Soirée*
- *Toast to Leap Year*

Cocktails with Art & Giada

Sudimack

A GORGEOUS COURTYARD provided the *Midsummer Night's Dream* setting for an al fresco summer cocktail party. Renowned chef and dear friend Art Smith was hosting "just a few" friends in his artfully adorned home to celebrate another beloved chef, friend Giada De Laurentiis', newest cookbook.

It was an elegant, decadent, and, of course, Italian party, thrown at home—which always creates the most intimate of gatherings. Guests arrived under a golden Chicago sunset sky and cocktailed in the incredible outdoor kitchen, sipping and snacking on Mediterranean cheese, olives, and toasts served in a wooden French cheese cave atop large, flat grape leaves. The smell of farm fresh *pizzettes* being cooked in an authentic wood-burning oven on the patio created the ultimate temptation to belly up to the antipasti bar.

Though outside it was a simple backyard party, inside among the various dining rooms created in the library, living room, and kitchen, the flowers were lush and opulent. Decadent blooms of crimson red, fuchsia, and jade green created a jewel-tone warmth that celebrated the *Everyday Italian* star's sparkling personality and heritage. One long patio table—added as the guest list grew up until the very last minute—was trimmed last minute with "instant" centerpieces in vintage glass trifle bowls with gorgeous, fresh-picked farm-to-table vegetables and herbs as centerpieces. It was simple and stunning—just as summer should be.

Soon, there was a toast to Giada, to her new best-selling book, and to all of her successes. Next, everyone moved inside to the kitchen, where an authentic Italian buffet awaited, with antipasti, fish and, of course, pasta, as well as a chocolate extravaganza for *dolce*, or dessert, marvelously prepared by the French Pastry School in Chicago.

Inside, the richly colored florals were interwoven as graceful garlands around Art's stunning wrought-iron candelabras. The personal collections and eclectic décor of Art's home were the guide and vision for the party—and became the inspiration for décor, centerpieces, and linens. The collection of artifacts became renaissance work-of-art centerpieces on a thirty-foot-long dining table set for the occasion in the living room. Handmade quilts, loaned from an artist friend in NYC, were repurposed and used as tablecloths in colorful, vibrant jewel tones. As always, we put candles everywhere, *everywhere* to create a warm, flickering ambience. The unbelievable floor-to-ceiling Latin art, compliments of Jesus Salguerio, Art's talented artist husband, set the tone for the evening. A favorite stylist tip: let your home décor be your guide for "the look" and color palette for the party.

The energy of an at-home party cannot be matched, and no other venue can compare. Guests love coming into one's home, taking a peek around, and learning about the host throwing the party. Not to mention, parties at home are often far less expensive, forgoing all rental fees.

This party was a gathering among friends, old and new. Mingling continued late into the evening, mixing Food Network execs with local foodies for fun. Guests moved from the outdoors to the indoors, and then back to the outdoors again, with nibbles on the buffet and cocktails flowing until late into the evening, when it was finally time to say, "*Ciao, bella!*"

Seasonal Savoir-Faire: When weather permits, transport your indoor furniture outside to create a festive seasonal cocktail garden for your guests and free up space for dining inside together. You'll enjoy the weather and the luxury of eating as one intimate group.

Go Green: Your home is full of centerpieces-in-waiting for dining and buffet tables. Take candelabra, candlesticks, beautiful pieces of sculpture, or interesting artifacts from your home and turn them into centerpieces. Add a few fresh flowers, embellish with some tall taper or votive candles, and voilà!—no need to buy and consume resources on new focal points for your party's décor. Repurpose, reuse, and recycle. Plus, guests just love to hear the interesting story of your collections, from acquisition to family heirloom.

Pizza Margarita from Chef Art Smith
Serves 6

Ingredients:
2 packages fresh pizza dough (I love healthy whole wheat, but you can also buy gluten-free.)
1 28-oz. can crushed tomatoes (San Marzano is a favorite)
1 lb. fresh mozzarella, sliced thin
olive oil to drizzle
fresh basil
fresh ground pepper

Preparation:
Simmer tomatoes over medium heat for 10 minutes. Shape each dough piece into a 1/4-inch-thick round and place on a cornmeal-covered baking sheet without sides. Put a thin layer of tomato and mozzarella on each round of pizza dough and sprinkle with olive oil and pepper. Bake for 7 to 8 minutes, or until the cheese has melted and the crust is golden. Tear the fresh basil onto the pizza and serve immediately.

Insalata di Rucola e Asparagi

from celebrity Chef Art Smith

Gluten Free! Serves 6

Ingredients:
vinaigrette
2 tbsp. balsamic vinegar
1 t. Dijon mustard
Salt and pepper to taste
6 tbsp. olive oil
1 medium shallot, finely chopped
1 t. chopped fresh thyme

Preparation:
In a medium bowl, whisk together the vinegar, mustard, salt, and pepper. Slowly drizzle in the oil, whisking constantly, until it comes together. Stir in the shallot and thyme. Taste for seasoning and add more salt and pepper.

Salad:
1 lb. asparagus, ends snapped off
2 small onions, halved
3 tbsp. olive oil
Salt and pepper, to taste
4 oz. goat cheese
1 t. chopped fresh thyme
1/2 lb. baby arugula

Preparation:
Heat grill. Toss the asparagus and onions with 1 tablespoon of the oil, and a generous

amount of salt and pepper. Grill the asparagus and onions, turning occasionally, for 6 to 10 minutes or until they brown. Let cool. Cut the asparagus into 2-inch pieces and slice the onion thinly. Toss the arugula with the asparagus, onions, and half of the vinaigrette. Arrange the salad on 6 plates and sprinkle with the remaining vinaigrette. Add fresh ground black pepper to garnish.

DIY #1: The Edible Centerpiece

Create an edible, organic centerpiece with nothing more than fruits, vegetables, and a few interesting containers you have lying around the house. As this party's guest list continued expanding up to the very last minute, we had to add additional tables inside, then even more outside. We quickly ran out of extra flowers—so we used these easy centerpieces outdoors. Edible centerpieces work anywhere and in any season.

Gather and count out your containers. A good-size bowl works for a table of four. Accent elements for buffets, bars, and side tables should be considered, too. Everything from bowls to vases to juice glasses works, as do wooden or metal pieces, so long as you keep the material consistent throughout the party.

Check that you have plenty of votive candles and purchase or borrow more if you don't.

Purchase your fresh fruits and/or vegetables, depending on what's in season and the theme of your party. Visit a farmer's market or a specialty food store to gather exotic produce. Or, visit the supermarket for fresh, simple fare.

Some design elements to consider: What is the theme of your party? Rustic or formal? Choose containers and produce accordingly. Do you want to mix fruits and vegetables or just choose from one? Will your containers have just one type or color of produce, or will you mix? Both approaches are lovely and can be used for different effects.

To create a fresh fruit, Italian-themed centerpiece, fill a low bowl with grapes, figs, and black berries, then tuck in clipped blooms of spray roses or orchids.

To create a fresh vegetable centerpiece, fill a sturdy wooden or ceramic bowl with kale or another leafy green, fresh tomatoes, and sprigs of fresh herbs.

For a simple year-round piece, fill a tall, clear vase with lemons.

For accent pieces, place single pieces of fresh fruit or vegetables on individual glasses. Space in a line down the center of a dining table or more randomly on a buffet table. Or, fill a crystal pedestal dish with key limes, cherry tomatoes, kumquats, or other petite fruits and vegetables.

Scatter your votive candles around the containers to create warmth.

Tomorrow: Make a fresh fruit or vegetable salad with your formerly fabulous centerpieces.

DIY #2: The Chocolate Shop Bar

Sometimes, dessert can seem like an afterthought. Make a sweet treat something to remember with a decadent buffet. Your guests will be inspired to get up (always good), talk with each other, and try new desserts in a way they might not with more a formal table service. An interactive dessert bar is a great way to kick up the energy level for your party mid-flight.

Arrange your dessert table before guests arrive. Bring out a collection of platters and, if you have them, cake stands. Use an eclectic mix of plates and tea and coffee cups for a special, but easy, look.

Serve bite-size desserts like cake pops, cake truffles, petite pies, mini-cupcakes, bite-sized tarts, and petite cookies. Family favorites are easily made tiny. Make old-fashioned recipes, but with a new twist, cut into bite-size pieces or portions.

To recreate the chocolate bar we did at this party, try an assortment of decadent truffles. Continue the sweetness with mini chocolate cakes and pie "shots," served in small glasses. Another lovely and easy dessert is to fill a trifle bowl with alternating layers of cake, fresh fruit and whipped cream, and serve in glasses.

Arrange your delicious desserts on cake stands and platters, and finish the table with scattered votive candles.

Winter Wonderland

A WONDROUS WHITE winter wonderland awaited more than 300 guests. The occasion? An über-chic corporate holiday party, thrown in Chicago's fabulous River East Arts Center, an old warehouse situated on the Chicago River in the heart of the city.

Guests arrived at the front door, welcomed by a group of carolers dressed in traditional Victorian garb, singing holiday favorites near the entrance. Once inside, a trio of three retro babes known during holiday season as "The Jingle Belles" performed a cappella holiday songs a la The Supremes in velvet and white fur collars. Guests were greeted with themed, specialty cocktails made just for the evening: Limoncello Ice-tinis chilled in a stunning tray of solid ice and topped with festive champagne gumdrops.

The entire décor was monocolor magnificence, with an elegant white-on-white palette from the tiniest to grandest detail. White silk linens set the backdrop. Stunning, frosted "iced" lanterns created a warm glow across

tabletops, bars, and outdoor terrace vistas. White winter flowers from amaryllis, phalaenopsis orchids, calla lilies, and hydrangeas brimmed from clear glass vases, dressed in strands of vertical sparkling chandelier crystals and white silk ribbon bands.

Accents of Moroccan gold and silver mercury glass tealights peppered the lofty landscape, including entertainment by live painted human statues, adding winter-themed "art" of yet another dimension to the gallery. The Snow Queen, Hip-Hop Jack Frost, and a Silver Celestial Moon glittered and vogued while posing. As guests moved throughout the party, they whispered, "Is that a statue? No, it's moving—it's a real person!"

Along with lemony gumdrop cocktails, guests enjoyed hors d'oeuvres like baby New Zealand lamb chops with cilantro dipping sauce, lobster salad in rice paper baskets, and blue cheese popovers with beef tenderloin and arugula.

Afterwards, everyone moved down to the submerged dining room, where the entertainment and the cuisine continued. Asian, Tex-Mex, and American food stations served maki rolls, truffled steak frites, handmade chicken tacos, and everything in between. An all-white "iced" candy bar beckoned guests from dinner to dessert with sweet treats including white chocolate malted milk balls, handmade champagne marshmallows, and saltwater taffy, all housed in vintage apothecary jars.

Performances changed every hour, on the hour, a la a turn of the century French cabaret. An a cappella doo wop quartet, AcRock, sang classic Jersey Boys–inspired rock 'n roll oldies in vivid neon costumes. Next, a Motown group, The Connection, brought the house down with toe tapping, finger snapping style, in vintage Zoot Suits, and Chicago's own legendary Second City comedy troupe performed a custom show written just for the guests in the group at the holidays. Last, a DJ took over and opened up the dance floor until the wee hours. A happy holiday was indeed had by all.

Haute Hostess: Why not skip the predictable traditional holiday décor and create unusual elegance this year instead? I just love this stunning wintry white-on-white palette. Another favorite on trend holiday color combination is apple green, white, and gold. Or, choose copper and aqua. Use this color scheme throughout your holiday details, from décor to holiday cocktails to menus to favors—even just adding in hints of new color through dozens of handmade silk bows to your mantle, tree, wreath, etc. These colors work beautifully both on the tabletop and for outdoor décor, too.

Asian Noodle Salad from J&L Catering

Gluten Free! Serves 6

Ingredients:
1 lb. rice noodles
4 tbsp. vegetable oil
1 tbsp. sesame oil
1 tbsp. hoisin sauce
2 t. chili paste
1 bunch fresh cilantro
1 bunch fresh basil
1 medium carrot
1 medium yellow onion
3 ribs celery
1 red pepper
1 yellow pepper
1 green pepper
1 cup bean sprouts
fresh ground black pepper to taste

Preparation:

Bring two quarts of water and two tablespoons of vegetable oil to a boil. Add noodles; cook until soft (3–5 minutes). Strain in a colander, run under cool water, gently pressing excess water from noodles. Place into a bowl. Gently toss noodles with sesame oil and pepper to taste. Julienne vegetables into strips but keep separate. Pre-heat a large sauté pan; add oil once hot. Sauté onion and carrot until al dente, then add the rest of the vegetables and sauté quickly. Set aside to cool. Wash herbs and roughly chop. Combine vegetables, noodles, herbs, hoisin, and chili paste in bowl; mix gently. Top with bean sprouts. Serve either buffet-style in a bowl or in mini Chinese takeout boxes with chopsticks. Serve with crushed peanuts, hoisin, soy sauce, or chili paste on the side.

Blue Cheese Beef Popovers

from J&L Catering Serves 12

Ingredients:

2 large eggs

1 cup milk

1 cup all-purpose flour
(can substitute gluten free flour)

1/2 t. salt

1/2 t. freshly ground black pepper

2 tbsp. melted butter

5 oz. blue cheese

1 pound thinly sliced beef tenderloin,
or rare roast beef

1 bunch fresh arugula

Preparation:

To make the popovers, whisk the eggs and milk together, then add the flour, salt, and pepper. Once blended, add the butter and blue cheese. Let sit for 20 minutes.

(Blue Cheese Beef Popovers continued)
Pour or scoop the mixture into well-greased full-size or miniature muffin pans. (The recipe makes 12 full-size popovers or 24 miniature popovers.) Bake at 350°F until brown. Let cool. Slice each popover 3/4 of the way through and fill with paper-thin slices of grilled beef tenderloin and an arugula leaf.

DIY #3: Winter's White Palette
Holiday décor can become tired and predictable with the usual traditional red and green decor. It's easy to transform this year's holiday celebration into an elegant, monochromatic, all white winter wonderland that works for any budget.

Make a statement on a tabletop, mantle, or kitchen island for a festive focal point throughout the holiday season. Fill vases and other containers with abundant white winter blooms. You can use any favorite bloom—from long lasting Amaryllis on one end of the price scale, to massed Carnations on the other end. Carnations are such a favorite of mine—grouped into a tight "pave" inside a vase, they make such an impact—and are so affordable. A floral stylist secret—the power of one flower creates a stunning effect. Buy several dozen, trim stems so that the base of your blooms are flush with the containers and fill them. Wrap white ribbon around into "bands," and secure with double sided tape or a glue stick. I love to drop a few crystal chandelier crystals off of the rim of the vase for a shot of sparkle at the holiday. And last, as always, mismatched containers with different shapes and heights are a favorite trick to add visual interest.

Create gorgeous, easy accents with spray-painted white and au naturale pinecones. On oversize sugar pinecones, accent with long, lingering silk ribbons. Scatter on mantles, tabletops, or arrange in baskets.

Dress the ultimate Christmas tree with accents of fresh flowers, like orchids, chrysanthemums, and tussie mussies of carnations, with your collection of elegant ornaments for shine and sparkle. Florals can be cut and water-tubed at the base of each stem for a long-lasting effect (available at your local florist or craft store).

DIY #4: Frosted Glass Centerpieces
Transform your glassware into festive holiday pieces with this simple, frosty stylist trick.

Gather glass bowls, hurricanes, and glass pieces of any size and shape.

Purchase one or more cans of spray frost at a craft store, florist, or hardware store.

In a well-ventilated area, preferably outside, spray your glass pieces as if you are spray-painting them on the outside of the glass. Allow to dry.

If your pieces do not look "frosted" enough, you can easily apply a second coat. It's ok to layer—the more layers—the frostier.

Fill with florals, pillar candles, and whatever strikes your winter fancy. The best news? You can wash off spray frost at the end of the holidays and continue putting those pieces to use long after, when spring has sprung.

A more permanent trick for vases and glass pieces is to spray-paint the interior with a colored paint. We used white for this party, but any great color works beautifully and gives the appearance of colored glass. By spray-painting just the inside, old glass pieces become newly colorful and glossy.

Spa Soirée

SPA SOIREE 2006

WE HOSTED THE ULTIMATE spa party to honor our top clients at the open-air Prairie Production, a beautiful photography studio loft in downtown Chicago. The idea on this day was to pamper, relax, and savor the moment.

As our special guests arrived, long pieces of gauzy white fabric billowed in the breeze. It was the perfect welcome to set the tone for relaxation. We transformed the normally empty loft into the most gorgeous "Zen" beachfront spa. Oversized cabanas, framed with crisp, white fabric, and oversize white lounge beds in the center beckoned guests to sit a spell. Lounge areas contained plush couches and modern coffee tables for guests to relax in between sips, bites, and of course—treatments.

Vintage lockers set the backdrop, with plenty of fluffy, rolled white towels. Chicago's bring-it-to-you anytime, anywhere spa service, *Beauty on Call*, offered a luxurious rotation of more than 20 treatments: microdermabrasion, pedicures, brow shaping, reflexology, and pro-

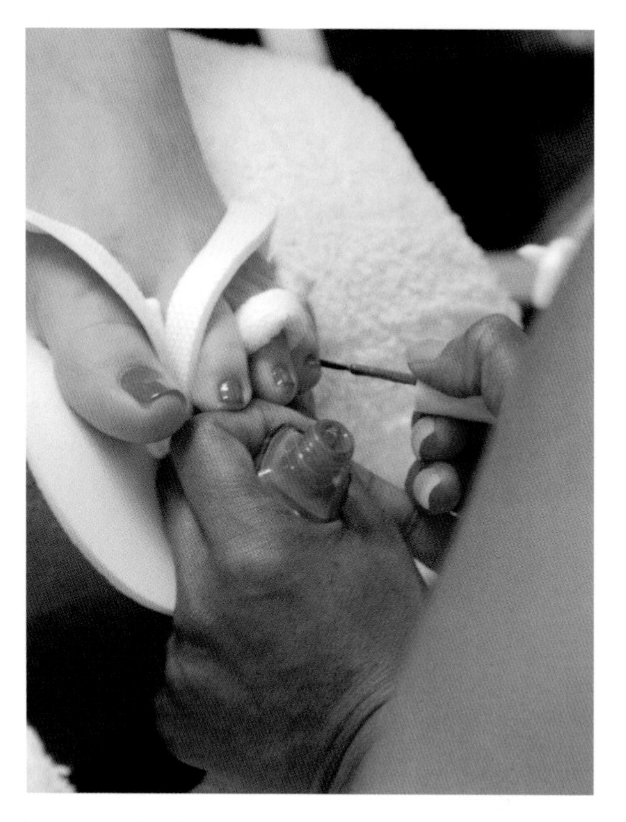

fessional shaves were just some of the indulgences on the spa menu.

Our flowers were even "Namaste." Gardenias, orchids, and calla lilies in simple glass collections showcased the soothing beauty of water and nature. Submerged glossy, green hosta leaves, one of my favorites and found in most backyards, were featured throughout the party on tabletops, floors, and more. Traditional round glass rose bowls were stacked in towers, and filled with single floating blooms in water, for interesting, modern centerpieces a la Georges V in Paris.

Guests were welcomed at the entrance with a fresh, minted warm towel, offered on a tray by an attendant—instantly "washing away" the day's work and stress. Mint is very soothing and relaxing with an aromatic scent, and a wonderful touch to start the party in a transporting way. "Spa-tinis" were served at the bar to loosen things up, with a nutritious kick, of course. We paired vodka with Airforce Nutrisodas, a healthy,

Little List: Here's how to plan the ultimate at-home spa party, and enjoy it as much as a day at the spa. Pamper yourself and your guests with this easy approach.

2 Months: Determine which spa services you will offer and book your aestheticians.

6 Weeks: Order or make your invitations. Be sure to tell your guests this is a party that's all about pampering.

1 Month: Mail invitations.

2 Weeks: Buy any supplies you may need for spa services and other decorative elements, such as glass rose bowls, vases, or floating candles. (See DIY #5.) Also get washcloths, nail polish, and other spa-treatment ingredients.

1 Week: Map out your spa stations. This can be as simple as an oversized chair for pedicures and facials, and the kitchen table for manicures. If the weather looks good, consider taking the party outside to the backyard.

3 Days: Set up your dining room table as the buffet and count out your glass pieces—e.g., small glasses for pea soup shooters, platters and trays for skewers and other food items, and glasses for drinks.

2 Days: Shop for all food and drink items. Set up your spa "stations" with all of the necessary pieces, from towels to lotion.

1 Day: Prepare your flower and leaf arrangements (See DIY #5). Remember, it's eclectic and simple. My party prep secret: prepare your entire menu, too, since all of the food can be made the day before and served at room temperature.

Day of: Assemble last-minute food items, set them out, and by gosh, relax and enjoy yourself.

all-natural soda available in a variety of flavors, with anti-oxidants and vitamins to boot. Each guest mosied up to the bar to pick his or her flavor—displayed in a colorful, cubist bar.

My favorite detail as guests arrived was the sunglasses washer. An attendant personally made sure that each guest's shades sparkled in the sun—again transporting us all to warmer, seaside climates far from Chicago.

The menu was simple and light. Healthy edibles like pea soup shooters, cantaloupe lollipops, fresh Caprese pops, and Ahi tuna lollipops were just the fuel needed to keep the beauty treatments coming. But what's a party without a little sweet indulgence? Dessert was a grand dark chocolate fondue bar, with the best of both worlds. A variety of dipping pieces included cookies, angel food cake, fresh fruit, dried fruits, and nuts. Guests who passed on the sweet, molten, antioxidant-rich chocolate still got to indulge in all of these wonderful, healthful treats—making it fun for everyone, and every diet.

Hip lounge music played gently in the background, and beauty—in every way from sight, taste, and sound—did abound.

The Spa-tini

This drink is so much fun. Airforce Nutrisodas come in small cans, in a variety of wonderful colors and flavors, each with a unique blend of vitamins, herbs and antioxidants. Guests can come up to the bar, choose from the variety (Calm, Radiant, Slender, and Renew, to name just a few), and place their order: I want a "Calm-tini" or I want a "Slender-tini." So delicious and nutritious!

Ingredients:
Grey Goose Vodka

Airforce Nutrisoda (can use any all natural, colorful "soda")

Preparation:
Combine 1 ounce of vodka with 2 ounces of Airforce Nutrisoda in a martini shaker filled with ice. Shake, pour, and enjoy. Garnish with fresh fruit. (I love slicing star fruit or key limes.)

Tuna Watermelon Skewers

by Food for Thought

Gluten Free!   Serves 6

Ingredients:

Skewers:

1/2 lb. Ahi tuna, sushi-grade
1/2 c. tamari
1/2 c. back and white sesame seeds, toasted
1/4 seedless watermelon
1/2 seedless cucumber
3 radishes

Lemon Coulis:

2 lemons
3/4 cup extra virgin olive oil
1/2 cup brown sugar
1/4 cup sea salt
freshly ground black pepper, to taste
10 bamboo skewers, about 4" long (often called Brochette skewers)

Preparation:

Dice the tuna into 3/4-inch cubes. Sprinkle each diced cube with tamari, extra virgin olive oil, and a few sesame seeds. Allow the tuna to marinate for a few minutes while you cut the seedless watermelon in 3/4-inch cubes to resemble the Ahi tuna. Slice the cucumber into 1/2-inch slices and cut slices into 4 equal-sized wedges. Using a mandolin, or very sharp knife, slice the radish as thin as possible while trying to maintain a nice and even round piece. Assemble the skewers, starting with a piece of watermelon, radish, tuna, and lastly, cucumber. For the lemon coulis, using a zester or grater, grate the skin of 2 lemons. Avoid grating the white pith of the lemon because of its bitter flavor. Juice both lemons as well and combine the juice with the zest, brown sugar, and the remainder of the extra virgin olive oil in a blender. Blend until emulsified. Season the coulis with salt and pepper. Just before serving, lightly drizzle the skewers with the lemon coulis and the toasted sesame seeds.

DIY #5: Submerged Hosta Centerpieces
The clean, elegant look of this party is as simple as water and leaves that you can find in your very own backyard (or a nice, sharing neighbor). Here's how to use nature's best elements and inexpensive glass vases to a stunning effect.

Assemble a collection of cylinder vases, floating candles, and three rose bowl vases, if you don't already have them. They are available at very affordable prices in most grocery, floral, and craft stores.

For cylinder vases, gather one hosta or long, narrow green leaf for each from the backyard or garden.

Fill cylinder vases three-fourths full with water. Submerge a leaf upside down in the water and place a floating candle on top of it, which will force the leaf to stay in place. The water and the glass will magnify the leaf exponentially, creating magical backyard beauty. Light the candle—and done.

For your rose bowl vases, gather large, flat, round blooms from the garden or purchase them. You only need three great blooms for this arrangement. My favorites include orchids, roses, or peonies.

Clip your blooms so that little, if any, stem remains.

Place one bloom in the bottom of one rose bowl and fill two-thirds with water.

Repeat with another bloom and rose bowl, but fill this one only halfway at most.

Repeat with the final bloom and rose bowl.

Toast to Leap Year

IMAGINE THE MOST beautiful, ethereal, elegant, soft as a cloud, feminine, French-inspired cocktail party.

Throw in the sparkle and celebration of the special occasion of an anniversary that falls on the very date of February 29th, layering into the excitement—Leap Year.

The occasion commemorated the beautiful and talented Elaina Vasquez, now owner of Chicago's Boutique Bites Catering...but whom just one Leap Year ago was chef extraordinaire at Joël Robuchon, MGM Grand in Las Vegas. Elaina had worked in several fine dining restaurants, and longed to bring the concept of restaurant-style food to catering. And voilà—as fate would have it—she was hired to cater a Leap Year party for very wealthy and influential guests in Las Vegas—including über chic

Brian Atwood, shoe designer extraordinaire. That night Boutique Bites was born.

Fast forward four years and one Leap Year, and Elaina created a gastronomic feast just for this magical evening—and feast guests did. Bringing together friends, family, industry partners, and media to toast in unison on February 29th, she created a roaming cocktail party with a savory tasting bar topped with tiered towers, almost a dozen glossy trays of tiny bite-size hors d'oeuvres, and finally a French patisserie creation—cleverly crafted as a sensational visual display in a book case.

Passed bites included: Foie French Toast (served to Brian Atwood himself at her very first party), Blinis and Caviar, Chicken and Waffles, Fish 'N Chips, 24K Deviled Quail Eggs, Mango Shrimp Lollipops, Shrimp Tempura Lollipops,

Lobster Tacos, Mini Chicago-Style Hot Dogs, and Corn Soup Shooters.

Savory Buffet displayed: Mini Cheeseburgers, Parmesan-Truffle Frites, Mini Milkshakes, Popcorn Chicken served in mini popcorn boxes, Mini Turkey and Swiss Tea Sandwiches paired with Chips.

Such daring food flavor—presented in such darling displays—all tasted divine. It was literally a feast for the senses paired with a trio of infused fruit and herb mixology cocktails, masses of white and blush Peonies and Hydrangea covering every tabletop, flickering votives, and pillar candles as far as the eye could see. In a Parisian Patisserie display were sweet treats and beautiful bites served on bookcase shelving, stacked on top of candlesticks, turned into instant cake stands. Petite pastry, macarons, citrus tarts, and more from Julius Meinl and Sugar Fixe Patisserie created the picture perfect pretty ending to an evening of sheer, reflective, celebratory bliss.

Mango Shrimp Lollipops

by Boutique Bites

Gluten Free!   Serves 12

Ingredients:

12 30/40 count (tip: means there are 30–40 shrimp in a pound) shrimp, peeled, and deveined
2 tbsp. white wine
1 tbsp. kosher salt
2 tbsp. olive oil
1 tbsp. lime juice
chile de arbol to taste (can substitute cayenne pepper)
1 mango

Avocado Puree:

1 avocado
1 tbsp. olive oil
1 t. lime juice
1 t. salt
12 lollipop sticks, 4.5"

Preparation:

In a pot large enough to hold shrimp, simmer water and add white wine and kosher salt.

Once water comes to a simmer, add shrimp and gently cook for 1 minute. Once shrimp is cooked, transfer to an ice bath to stop cooking. Drain well and pat dry. Marinate with remaining olive oil, lime juice, chile de arbol, and salt to taste. Peel mango and dice into 1-inch cubes. For the avocado puree, halve and peel avocado. Dice and puree in food processor with olive oil and lime juice until smooth. Add salt to taste. To assemble, skewer mango and shrimp through lollipop stick. Top with avocado puree.

Popcorn Chicken (served in mini popcorn boxes)

by Boutique Bites

Serves 12

Ingredients:

6 boneless skinless chicken breasts
2 cups buttermilk
1 t. Old Bay seasoning
1 tbsp. kosher salt
2 eggs, beaten
2 cups all purpose flour, seasoned with salt & pepper
1 quart corn oil to fry
12 mini popcorn boxes (from Party Store)
1 box low-sodium all natural microwave popcorn, popped

Preparation:

Marinate chicken breasts in the buttermilk seasoned with Old Bay and kosher salt for 6 hours. Remove chicken from marinade and pat dry. Cut into cubes. Add to flour. Add to egg, add back to flour. Fry in pan with oil heated to 350, in small batches, till brown. Drain. Keep warm in oven. Fill popcorn boxes with chicken and popcorn mixture. Serve warm.

chapter two

DINNER IS SERVED

WHAT COULD BE BETTER than getting together with friends and loved ones for an evening of food, drink, and spirited celebration? I love a dinner party for all of its potential. Whether for a special occasion or *simply because*, everything and anything goes at a dinner party.

A fabulous dinner party can be whipped up in seconds (order Thai food from the local take-out, phone friends, buy delicious wine, light candles...and voilà!), or a dinner party can be a truly grand affair. When you want to celebrate something—or someone—special, it's all about the chic, personal touch. One golden thread carried throughout the evening weaves your very own perfect dinner party.

Whatever your occasion, a great dinner party is waiting. The celebrations in the pages that follow will provide you with plenty of inspiration. Sumptuous food, a specialty cocktail, and one or two personalized, thoughtful touches are all you need to host a festive night to remember.

In this chapter you'll find:

- *An Oscar Dinner*
- *A Fabulous, French Affair*
- *A Retirement Dinner*

An Oscar Dinner

STUNNING GOLDS, WARM CORALS, and a luscious feast set the tone for an evening fit for a gilded king. Guests were celebrating a Hollywood nomination for an Academy-Award-winning performance in the year's top film. A small, intimate group of 25 gathered at a private at-home affair in sunny California, the estate set against the backdrop of the Pacific Ocean for an intimate dinner party. The beautiful hue of Oscar-statuette gold set the theme for the entire evening.

Guests were greeted with an "Oscar-tini" upon arrival in the living room, created by mixologists for the guest of honor and the evening ahead. A drink menu was printed and set in a frame (Oscar gold, of course) atop the bar.

After cocktailing, guests continued on to an outdoor veranda. We tented the veranda with gorgeous gold drapery, which were sheer and lovely, so guests couldn't see the tenting mechanics and structure above them.

Seasonal Vegetable Stew with Cous Cous Pilaf
Roasted Free Range Chicken Breasts with Wild Mushroom Ragu
White Truffle Risotto with Peas, Spinach and Soy Beans
Grilled Seasonal Vegetables or Gratin of Vegetables
Salad of Promise Land Greens, Dried Apricots, Apples and Parmesan Cheese with Mustard Dressing
Art's Foccacia
Hummingbird Cake, Ambrosia, Fresh Fruit Sorbets
Auntie Chocolate Cake with Fudge Sauce
Red Velvet Cake
Coffee and Tea Service
Homemade Candy
February 2, 2007

We designed one long, European dining table, which added to the feeling of intimacy for this among-friends celebration. Corals and golds danced along the tabletop, and low florals and lavish candlelight finished the effect. Flowers well below eye level maintained a feeling of intimacy. Mango calla lilies and mokara and cymbidium orchids were arranged in hues of honey, tangerine, and copper, and housed in square and rectangular modern vases. Custom raw silk table linens with corner kickpleats and chair-back covers cocooned guests in a perfect, golden California night.

The beauty of this dinner party was in the variety. We'd gilded the vases with gold leaf for a lovely, warm effect that was also aged and imperfect. Votives in amber glass, more gilded gold, and Moroccan glass finished a tabletop that was a thoughtful, inspired collection of mixed metallic. This is one of my favorite design secrets—making the table more interesting to the eye, not to

mention more unique and eclectic for guests.

For dinner, we used exquisite, hand-embroidered hemstitch linen. The napkins featured personal initials, with a crown embroidered above them. (After all, he *was* king for the evening.) Tucked inside was the evening's menu, finished with a fresh orchid at each place setting. These layered elements provided a thoughtful touch for both guest of honor, and guests alike.

The menu was designed around personal favorite flavors, but with options for everyone, which is always highly recommended. The guest of honor is a vegan, so we served a variety of delicious dishes with fresh vegetables and wonderful sauces, but also some sinfully tasty meat and dairy for good measure.

After dinner, guests were greeted with a magnificent two-foot-tall Oscar statuette cake, hand-painted in gold. It was the *pièce de résistance*. Towering sparkler candles were lit in celebration. An indulgent dessert buffet featured celebrity baker Sam Godfrey's Red Velvet Cake.

Guests were farewelled with mini-Oscar cakes, in ribbon-wrapped acrylic boxes with a tag of the evening's signature icon and the date. It was a delightful final touch and a thoughtful surprise that completed the evening.

Seasonal Savoir-Faire: The evening featured all locally grown, seasonal California flowers to make the event truly of-the-moment. Our color palette was designed around in-season florals, which helps make any party special, affordable, *and* green. Your local florist should always be able to recommend what's in season, or what will be in season if you're planning in advance.

Red Velvet Cake

from Baker to the stars Sam Godfrey

Serves 6

Ingredients:

Cake:

2 1/4 cups sifted cake flour
(can use gluten free flour)
2 tbsp. unsweetened cocoa powder
1 t. baking powder
1 t. baking soda
1/2 t. salt
1 cup buttermilk
1 tbsp. red food coloring
1 t. distilled white vinegar
1 t. vanilla extract
1 1/2 cups sugar
1/2 cup (1 stick) unsalted butter,
room temperature
2 large eggs

Frosting:

2 8-oz. packages cream cheese,
room temperature
1/2 cup (1 stick) unsalted butter,
room temperature
1 tbsp. vanilla extract
2 1/2 cups powdered sugar

Preparation:

For cake: Preheat oven to 350°F. Butter and flour two 9-inch-diameter cake pans. Measure sifted flour, cocoa powder, baking powder, baking soda, and salt into medium bowl. Whisk buttermilk, food coloring, vinegar, and vanilla in small bowl to blend. Using electric mixer, beat sugar and butter in large bowl until well blended. Add eggs 1 at a time, beating until well blended after each addition. Beat in dry ingredients, alternating with buttermilk mixture in 3 additions. Divide batter between prepared pans. Bake cakes until tester inserted into center comes out clean, about 30 minutes. Cool in pans on racks for 10 minutes. Turn cakes out onto racks; cool completely.

For frosting: Beat cream cheese and butter in large bowl until smooth. Add vanilla. Mix in powdered sugar and beat until smooth. Spread frosting onto cooled cakes. Cake may be made and assembled one day in advance. Keep refrigerated.

The Oscar-tini
Serves 6

Ingredients:
Grey Goose vodka
Fresh lemon juice from Meyer lemons
(Party secret: Try Meyer lemon juice concentrate, all-natural and far less work)
1 lemon, sliced thin into rounds
1 bag, hard lemon candies

Preparation:
Combine 1 ounce of vodka with 1 ounce of lemon juice in a martini shaker filled with ice. Shake, pour and enjoy. Garnish with a floating lemon slice. For an extravagant touch, finish the cocktail with a sprinkling of 24-karat gold flecks. For a whimsical effect, drop in a lemon hard candy.

DIY #6: Monogrammed Napkin
Take a celebration to the next level with monogrammed napkins. I promise you don't have to be an expert seamstress to do it. Silk-ribbon embroidery started in 18th-century France. It's antiquey and romantic. You can create a custom monogram on your computer, and have an embroiderer do the work for you. Or, a more affordable option is using a rubber stamp and fabric ink pad.

Purchase linen or cotton napkins at your favorite home store.

Design a custom monogram or icon for the party on your computer, and have a rubber stamp made at an office supply store, printer, or stationery store.

Decide your embroidery or ink colors. You can do one color or several coordinating colors for each letter in a modern, two- or three-letter block monogram.

Place the rubber stamp onto the ink pad, then directly onto the napkins, keeping the stamp nice and straight. Allow to dry before stacking.

DIY #7: Gilded and Glorious Tablewares
Add the Midas touch to your next party with gilded, *easy* vases, votives, lanterns, and more.

Buy booklets of gold leaf, glass votive holders and vases, and 3M spray adhesive at your local craft store. Gold leaf is generally sold in booklets of 3″ x 3″ squares, which are very delicate.

Spray the outside of the glass votive or vase with adhesive.

Apply sheets of gold leaf randomly, leaving space and creating interest from one square to the next. Repeat. (The sprayed parts of the glass that are not covered with gold leaf will dry and not be sticky.)

Fill vase with water, arrange flowers. A candle will glow through the uncovered parts of the votive and light up the reflective, romantic gold-leaf.

You can use this gilding technique on just about anything: ceramic, metal, etc. Try it on affordable frames to make them extraordinary in an instant.

A Fabulous, French Affair

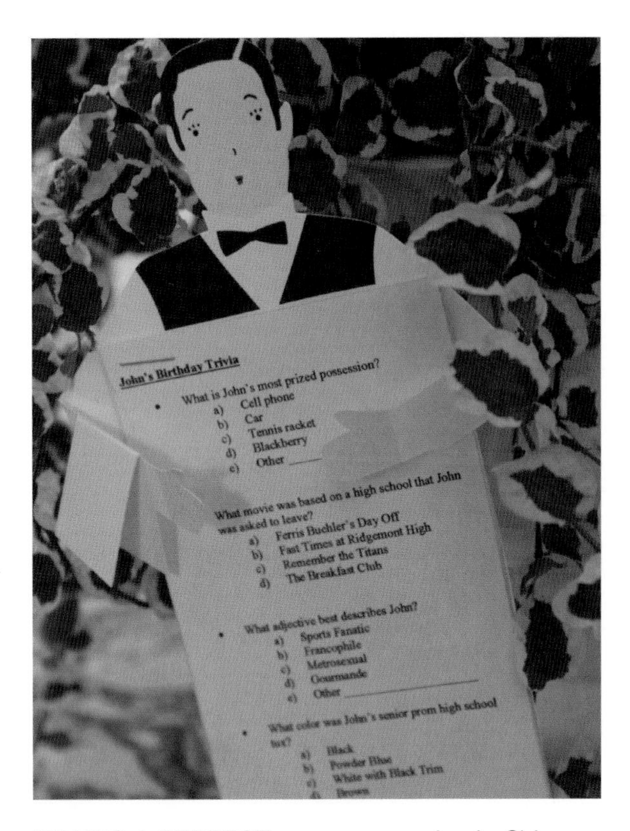

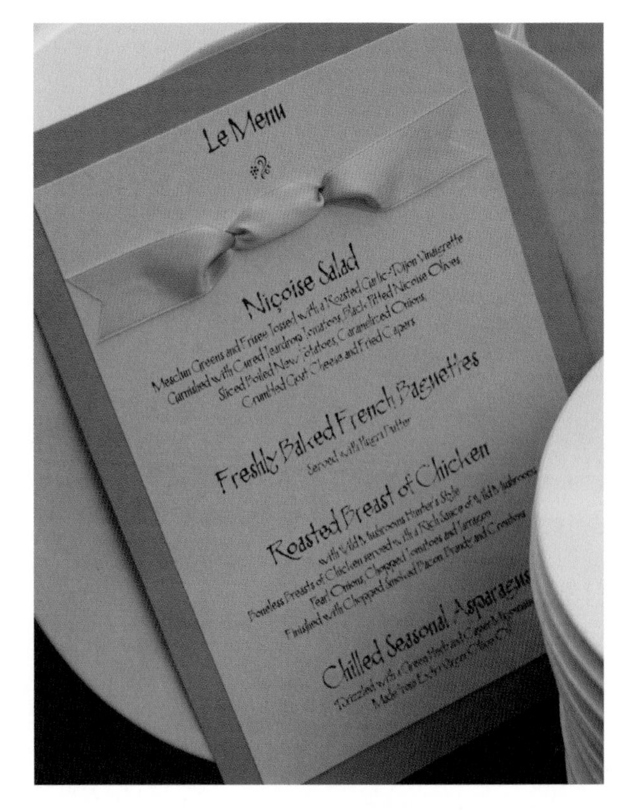

IT WAS A PERFECT summer evening in Chicago. Anyone who lives in Chicago knows that counting on the weather to cooperate, even in the summer, is a fifty-fifty gamble. However, on this night all of the stars were aligned for a spectacular backyard party in celebration of the season.

The theme of the evening was all-things-French *and* all-things-wine. Guests arrived for cocktails in the backyard, while a sommelier set up shop for a very French wine tasting. Soon after arriving, guests migrated to the table where they were educated on the guest of honor's favorite French wines. Regional and grape information was provided as guests swirled and sipped away on three reds and three whites.

Strawberries were halved, and served after de-stemmed, with soft cheese and balsamic vinegar and passed to guests. A decadent cheese plate of brie, bucheron, and bleu were nestled with grapes and fresh-baked French bread.

After the wine tasting, guests were seated

at tables draped in a gorgeous silk toile overlay, in a traditional cream and French blue. The centerpieces were fresh, aromatic lavender plantings in large stone urns. This is a traditional nod to the French fields—and is easy to assemble, and long lasting.

In keeping with a fun theme, guests had received a three-dimensional maître'd invitation that stood on its own and announced the party. This amazing meal was all about delicious, authentic French bistro food. Chefs prepared fresh steak *au poivre* on barbeques, and pommes frites, white and sweet potato, served in paper cones with mayonnaise. A niçoise salad was truly extraordinary, with caramelized onions, fresh grilled tuna, fried capers, and goat cheese.

But the birthday cake was the most fun of all. A fabulous three-tiered square cake with the Eiffel Tower on top, in the same French blue, celebrated the *Bonne Anniversaire*.

Fabulous, French, and fun.

Go Green: Lavender plantings were the dinner party centerpieces, which guests were to told to take home with them afterwards as a party favor. Rather than investing in cut flower centerpieces that don't have purpose at the end of the evening, try plantings that continue to thrive land bring new life long after the event. They're beautiful and commemorative.

Little List: Once the invitations have been sent, here's how to ensure smooth sailing until the moment your guests arrive.

1 Week: Purchase nonperishable food and wine (crackers, bottled goods, potatoes). Order cake.

3 Days: De-bug the yard. Purchase all remaining food (meats, cheeses, vegetables). Weather check for party day with an indoor plan B.

2 Days: Plant herbal centerpieces. Check weather.

1 Day: Food preparation (the key to enjoying yourself tomorrow). Wash and chop vegetables. Prepare herb butter. Ready meats and tuna for grilling.

Day of (in the morning): Final weather check—decide indoor or outdoor. Purchase French bread. Set tables. Chill wine. Prepare the cheese plate—room temperature, please. Hand off the cooking (it doesn't have to be a pro, but relieving yourself of this duty will allow you to enjoy your party). Voilà! You're done.

Niçoise Salad with Fresh-Grilled Tuna

from Food for Thought Catering

Gluten Free! Serves 6

Ingredients:

Dressing:

1/2 cup extra-virgin olive oil
3 tbsp. white wine vinegar
2 t. Dijon mustard
1 large garlic clove, minced
1/2 t. anchovy paste
salt and freshly ground black pepper to taste

Salad:

1 1/2 lb. new potatoes
1 1/2 lb. tuna steaks (1-inch-thick)
1/4 cup extra-virgin olive oil, plus extra for brushing tuna
1/4 cup bottled capers, drained
3/4 lb. mesclun and frisée greens
1 medium onion, sliced
2/3 cup bottled sundried tomatoes, drained
2/3 cup niçoise olives, pitted
3 tbsp. butter
1/3 cup chopped flat-leaf parsley

Preparation:

In a small bowl, whisk together dressing ingredients and set aside. Add potatoes to boiling water and simmer, uncovered, until tender, 15 to 20 minutes, then drain in a colander. Slice into 1/4-inch pieces once

cooled. While potatoes are cooking, heat oil in a 12-inch heavy skillet over moderate heat until hot but not smoking, and fry capers until slightly crisp and golden brown, about 3 minutes. Transfer capers with a slotted spoon to paper towels to drain. In a second skillet, melt butter over moderate-high heat. Add onions, stirring to coat with the melted butter. Add a pinch of salt. Continue cooking until the onions turn a golden brown, about 15 minutes. Lower heat slightly and cook until onions achieve a deeper brown color (this is the caramelization)—about 10 more minutes. Set aside. Brush tuna with oil and season with salt and pepper, then grill on lightly oiled rack, uncovered, turning over once, until browned on outside but still pink in center, 6 to 8 minutes total. Let tuna stand 3 minutes, then break into large pieces and drizzle with 1/3 of dressing. Toss greens and tomatoes with 1/3 of dressing. In a separate bowl, toss sliced potatoes with final 1/3 of dressing. Layer ingredients on a platter, using all of the potatoes as the bottom layer. In the middle, add lettuce and tomatoes, layered in with caramelized onions, olives, and fried capers. Finish with a heap of onions, olives, and capers, and add tuna and crumbled chevre to the top. Sprinkle with parsley.

PARTY TIP: French Wine, from Budget to Blasphemous

Budget ($12 and under)

2005 Joseph Drouhin La Foret Bourgogne Chardonnay Reserve
2005 Domaine Frissant Sauvignon
2004 Mouton Cadet Bordeaux, Baron Philippe de Rothschild
2003 Guigal Côtes du Rhône
2003 Jean-Philippe Janoueix Bordeaux
2004 Heron Pinot Noir

Bearable ($15–$40)

2001 Château Smith-Haut-Lafitte Blanc
2004 Verget Burgundy White Terroir de Chablis
2004 Château Moncontour Vouvray
2004 Patrick Lesec Châteauneuf du Pape "Pierres Dorees"
2004 Abbaye de Tholomies Minervois
2000 Château Cadet Piola Bordeaux

Blasphemous ($75+)

2004 Bernard Dugat-Py Meursault Vieilles Vignes
2002 Puligny-Montrachet Premier Cru
2003 Louis Latour Corton-Charlemagne Grand Cru
2003 Pavillion Rouge du Château Margaux
1996 Léoville-Poyferré
2001 Paul Jaboulet Aîné Hermitage La Chapelle

Retirement Dinner

Flying is done largely
with the
Imagination

HOW BETTER TO CELEBRATE a wonderful career than at Chicago's renowned Spiaggia restaurant, overlooking the Magnificent Mile with Lake Michigan sparkling in the background? A retiring pilot gathered with forty family and friends to celebrate the close of a remarkable career that had taken him around the world and back again, hundreds of times over.

As guests arrived, they were greeted with towering and festive display of Louis Vuitton steamer trunks, nearly six feet tall. The trunks opened to reveal wonderful photos from the Captain's storied career, from around the world and throughout his life. Embossed leather passport cases were lined across the steamer trunks in alphabetical order, serving as tablecards for the guests. Table names were travel-themed and upon finding their dinner table, were completed with a thoughtful travel quote.

Upon arrival, guests toasted and mingled with

a Spiced Pear Bellini from Top Chef Tony Mantuano. On each of the cocktail tables, whimsical centerpieces of vintage tin airplanes flew atop a "cloud" of fresh hydrangea, under a dome of a big glass cloche, surrounded by flickering votive candles.

Long, European banquet tables adorned with a global theme in rich, deep chocolate browns created a night to remember. Masculine was Captain's orders. Once at the table, guests found personalized luggage tags as placecards. Louis Vuitton once again dressed the tables, with mini-suitcases adorned with vintage travel and hotel seals from all of the Captain's favorite places: Prague, Martinique, and Italia, just to name a few. Vintage travel accessories like pencil cups, and antique globes served as bud vases, filled with florals and tucked in between the centerpieces.

And the food? Well, that the menu was sublime goes without saying. Chef Mantuano's

award-winning cuisine had guests enjoying the freshest Italian fish, succulent filet mignon, and homemade gnocchi. Beaded charger plates floated on the evening's menu, a calligraphied globe design, personalized for each guest.

After toasting and feasting, guests were treated to *Miniature Worldly Edibles*. Three custom-designed travel themed cakes were served around the table to guests. It made for a stunning *wow* as guests looked down the table and saw a succession of cakes: Louis Vuitton inspired luggage cakes, globe cakes, and miniature airplanes atop clouds of cake.

The night took guests on a beautiful flight, reflecting on a wonderful career, without ever leaving the ground.

Haute Hostess: What's the difference between a tablecard and a placecard? A tablecard directs guests to the table they are seated at, usually found with your name and table number or name as you enter an event. A placecard is found at the table and indicates your seat. Both cards add a thoughtful, finishing touch to entertaining and can be handwritten, printed on the computer, or calligraphied for a more formal look.

Spiced Pear Bellini

from Chef Tony Mantuano

Serves 6

Ingredients:
8 oz. pear nectar, chilled
2 bottles of prosecco, chilled (750 ml)
1/2 cup pear puree

Preparation:
Make pear puree: Preheat oven to 400°F. Peel, core, and halve two ripe pears. Arrange in a shallow baking dish and sprinkle with lemon juice, cinnamon, and allspice. Pour in 1/4 cup of orange juice. Bake for 30 minutes. Cool. Puree in a blender or food processor. Fill the bottom of a champagne glass with one tablespoon of pear puree and 1 ounce of pear nectar. Finish with prosecco.

Sorbet Tartlets

Serves 6

Ingredients:
Tart shells
(available in the freezer section of your grocery store)
1 pint sorbet, or varied flavors of sorbet
Berries
Mint leaves

Preparation:
Bake tartlet shells according to instructions the day of your party, and set aside. Scoop sorbet into each tartlet shell. Place tartlets on a baking sheet, wrap, and place in freezer until ready to serve. When guests arrive, you can plate on a single tray or on individual plates, and garnish with berries and mint leaves.

DIY #8

DIY #8: Vases Vases Everywhere

It's true—several items around your house are vases waiting to be transformed. Everyday objects can hold your flowers—water and all—and add a unique touch to any celebration. A favorite casual look is a brown or white paper lunch bag. That's right. Ready to learn?

Choose your florals. Pick what you want to use around the house as a vase (remember it's only temporary). Ideas include anything with a hollow space inside, such as pencil cups from desk accessories, canisters from the kitchen, small tote bags, antique tins, hat boxes, and more.

Place a drinking glass inside the chosen container to create a waterproof lining. Fill with water, about an inch from the top rim, so there is room for the florals without spilling.

Trim your flower stems at an angle, with the length to sit at the very top of the container. Place flower(s) into your new "vases." You can create bud vases, with simply one flower, or traditional arrangements with several.

DIY #9: The Customized Placesetting

The dinner party menu can be as tantalizing to the eye as it is to the palate. Try a custom menu set underneath a clear charger plate, for a look your guests will love.

Purchase clear glass plates or charger plates (larger in size, about 12 inches). Determine the diameter of the plate, by measuring only the base that sits flat on the table. This will be the diameter of your printed paper menu. Charger plates with bases measuring greater than 8" will need to be sent out for printing. Keep this in mind as you make your choice.

If you are printing the menus yourself, purchase lightweight card stock in a color that coordinates with your planned tabletop.

Design your menu on your computer, using Microsoft Word. In the "Page Set-Up" of your document (usually under "File"), choose the 8.5 x 11 paper option and change all margins to 0, so the design prints to the edge of the page.

Center your text and type up your menu, including your dinner wines, first course, salad, main entrée(s) and dessert. I love to include ingredient descriptions so guests are aware, in case of any allergies or dietary issues. Title your menu (John's 50th Dinner Celebration) and add customized touches throughout (John's Favorite Panzanella; John's Mother's Chocolate Ganache Cake, etc.).

Other elements to customize include: Text color, font type, and artwork. Insert a personal picture from your computer or a decorative piece of clip art. To create a watermark as your menu background, choose "Format," "Background" and "Picture Watermark." Select the picture you would like to use from your computer's hard drive. Adjust the size by changing the percentage under "Scale." It may take a few tries.

Print your menu. (Make sure to print one as a test on extra paper). Make sure your printer is set-up for the correct size paper and choose the highest quality ink setting (usually found in the Print window under "Properties").

Or, take your file to a stationery or print shop like Kinko's and have it printed there.

Once all of your menus are printed, place your clear charger plate onto each, ensuring the text is centered, and trace around it with a pencil.

Cut your menus into circles with a good quality scissors.

Place menus beneath charger plates on your lovely tabletop—and voilà.

Visit www.aperfectevent.com/inspirations for event invitation, menu and placecard templates.

chapter three

BIRTHDAY FÊTES

A BIRTHDAY PARTY is about so much more than a birthday cake. It's a magical opportunity to make our loved ones feel special—feel loved. When else does one person become the all important—stop the world—center of attention? It only happens once a year and great occasions are meant to be celebrated.

In this chapter you'll find:

- *Windy City 40th*
- *Dinner in Paris*
- *A Taste of Tuscany*
- *Birthday Times Two*

Whether a grand celebration or a small, cozy family gathering, a birthday party becomes a celebration to remember when you add a thoughtful, personal, special touch. It's easy to infuse your party details with the guest of honor. From the invitations to the menu and everything in between, here's how to make your next birthday party a celebration of life, love...and, yes, by golly, another notch on the life calendar.

A Windy City 40th

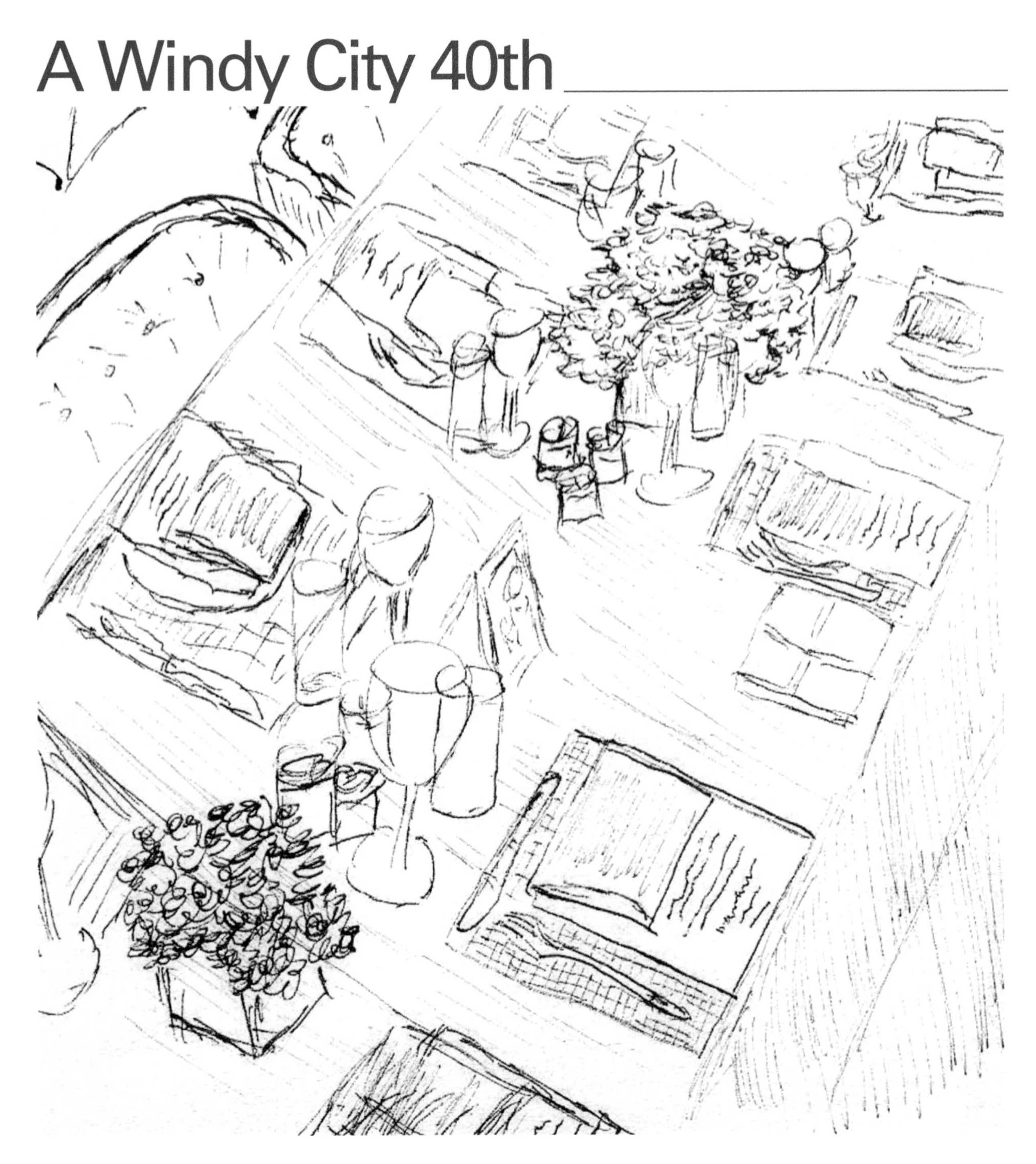

IT WAS A BIRTHDAY to remember—the big 4–0—thrown by a loving wife for her handsome husband and sixty of their closest friends. Every detail of this hipster, happy birthday party was designed around the guest of honor and his lovable, hilarious personality.

The party took place at Boka, the couple's dining room away from home—their favorite local restaurant—located just across the street from their home in the Old Town neighborhood of Chicago. Guests arrived at the tented courtyard, where all of the birthday boy's favorite hometown memorabilia provided plenty of conversation and reflective celebration. His favorite martini cocktail, named for the birthday boy, of course, and served as guests entered, got the good times rolling. Guests were invited to make their mark on a "this is your life" oversized frame, a fun, interactive version of a birthday-party guest book. After the party, it became

a coveted piece of artwork to remember the event.

Best of all, we celebrated the guests of honor's most beloved sayings, called "Panko-isms" by his close friends and family. Ten of the best were selected and printed on custom printed apple green cocktail napkins, the crisp color of the evening—paired with sleek urban black. The servers wore custom t-shirts, too, with the "Top Ten" printed on the back and a calendar picture from the birthday boy's fraternity days printed on the front.

Inside the restaurant, waves of nautical white canvas stretched across the ceiling, while hundreds of flickering candles gave the room a warm glow. The same gorgeous green and black hues gave a masculine touch to the party. Sleek, massed green cymbidium orchids, green hydrangeas, and

green jade roses were arranged monofloral, monocolor, in industrial black ceramic rectangular vases for a modern design.

Tabletop pictures of the birthday boy through the years were interspersed amongst the floral arrangements. Each guest found a custom-made CD at their placesetting, featuring all of "Panko's Greatest Hits." The same fraternity-calendar picture was on the cover, with the history or meaning of each song lovingly detailed on the back by his wife.

Boka Chef Giuseppe Tentori prepared an amazing small plate, farm-to-table tasting menu for guests. The first course was fettuccini with wild mushrooms and parmigiano reggiano. The second a field greens salad, with winter vegetables. For the main entree, guests had a choice of whitefish with bacon, corn, and potato chowder; braised pork shank with preserved tomato, niçoise olive, and potato puree; or roasted duck with persimmons, fourme d'ambert cheese, and aged balsamic.

During the last course, everyone watched a short "this is your life" film that celebrated the occasion and sang "Happy Birthday" with an oversized cake from his favorite bakery. A dessert bar featuring fun finger-foods kept guests noshing and dancing to a DJ through the night. Finally, it was time to say goodbye and guests were sent off with a bag of "Steve's Favorite Late-Night Munchies": a hot, fresh Krispy Kreme donut and cold Milk Chug in custom to-go bags.

> **Haute Hostess:** Who doesn't love a parting gift? Give guests a snack-to-go at the end of your next party and they're sure to leave surprised, and sweetly satisfied for the ride home. It can be as simple as a custom printed, chilled bottle of water or hot coffee to-go or as elaborate as warm "drinking" chocolate paired with a heavenly truffle brownie. Chances are, they'll enjoy it no matter what treat you tuck inside.

Butternut Squash Soup Shots

from Chef Giuseppe Tentori

Gluten Free!

Serves 12 in shot glasses

Ingredients:

1 large butternut squash, halved, seeds removed
6 tbsp. butter
Salt and pepper, to taste
3 carrots, minced
3 celery stalks, minced
1 small onion, minced
6 tbsp. vegetable oil
1/2 cup apple cider
3 cups chicken stock
1/4 t. fresh thyme
1/4 cup half and half
3 stems parsley, minced

Preparation:

Cut squash in half, remove seeds. Preheat oven to 350°. Put squash on baking sheet and dab 1 tablespoon of butter on each half. Sprinkle with salt and pepper. Bake for 45 minutes. In a large sauce pot, combine carrots, celery, and onions. Add 1 t. vegetable oil. Cook vegetables until translucent and tender. Add apple cider, chicken stock, thyme, salt, and pepper and simmer for 30 minutes. When squash is cool enough to handle, scoop out the flesh and add to simmering stock. Simmer until soup thickens, for 30 minutes. Remove from heat, and cool, until easy to handle. Put the soup into a blender to make creamy and smooth. Reheat soup and add half and half until piping hot. Serve in shot glasses, with a pinch of fresh parsley. Garnish with fresh pepper.

Note: I love to keep in a teapot warming in the microwave, and pour into shot glasses or espresso cups as guests arrive.

Tenderloin Toasts
from Chef Giuseppe Tentori

Ingredients:
French baguettes cut into on
the diagonal 1/4-inch slices
3 tbsp olive oil
2 tbsp white horseradish
1 1/2 lbs beef tenderloin
(have butcher trim and prepare for you at the counter)
course sea salt
1 tbsp brined green peppercorns
2 garlic cloves, minced
crushed red pepper flakes, to taste
1 tbsp fresh tarragon, minced
8 sliced green onions
1/2 c whipped cream cheese, at room temp
1 t. red pepper flakes
1 t. horseradish

Preparation:
Preheat oven to 400°F. Allow beef to come to room temperature, about 30 minutes. In a small bowl, combine tarragon, green peppercorns, garlic, sliced green onions, and a pinch of salt. Spread the mixture out on a baking sheet or platter large enough to fit the tenderloin. Brush olive oil on all sides of the beef tenderloin. Roll the beef in the pepper mixture to form a crust. In a large, ovenproof nonstick pan on a high heat setting, warm 2 tablespoons of olive oil. Add the tenderloin, and quickly sear until browned on all sides, about 3 minutes. Place in the oven and cook. After 15 minutes check the thickest part of the fillet with a sharp knife to see level of "pink" is correct. Transfer beef to a piece of aluminum foil, wrap, and let cool. Wrap the beef in foil, and put in the fridge for at least 3 hours. Reduce oven temperature to 300°F. Arrange the baguette slices in a single layer on a baking sheet. Place in the oven and toast until golden brown, 15 minutes total. Remove and let cool. In a bowl, whisk together cream cheese (bring to room temperature for easy mixing), red pepper flakes, horseradish. Remove the beef from the refrigerator, unwrap and slice against the grain as thinly as possible (having it cold helps the slices remain thin). Place a slice beef on the toast. Add a dollop of horseradish cream cheese.

DIY #10: Cocktail Napkins with Personality
Celebrate your birthday guy or gal with words of love, humorous sayings, or a party icon or logo to make cocktail napkins something to remember. It's easy to customize this pretty little party detail.

Brainstorm what saying(s) or message you will put on your cocktail napkins, in ten words or fewer. Choose one saying, or choose several.

Your napkins can be professionally printed at a stationery printer or online outlet, or, make your own by typesetting the saying/logo, and then ordering a custom rubber stamp for each saying or message. These are available at stationery and office supply stores.

Purchase stamp pad(s) in the coordinating party color. Consider the ink color you will be using and make sure it is significantly darker, if choosing light-colored napkins, or significantly lighter, if choosing dark-colored napkins.

Purchase cocktail napkins that coordinate with your party's theme and/or design. Buy five napkins per guest to make sure you have enough for the bar, cocktails, dessert.

At least one day before the party, create your napkins by firmly pressing your rubber stamp onto the stamp pad and then onto the napkin. Allow enough space for napkins to dry for an hour before stacking them.

Dinner in Paris

MAMIE'S BIRTHDAY MENU

ONE THOUGHTFUL, KIND HUSBAND, in speaking of his wife's upcoming birthday to her dear friend, said simply: "She doesn't want a party. She just wants to go out for a nice dinner, the two of us."

Said girlfriend, knowing full well what women really want, said, without hesitation: "Oh no, we are throwing her a party. A surprise party. And Debi Lilly will take care of everything."

LOVE HER.

What the wonderful, romantic husband really wanted to do was fly their ten closest friends to Paris, for the night, for dinner. But, as those with holiday birthdays know, celebrating in December can be a challenge, and travel schedules simply didn't allow for such a trip. Well, I know a thing or two about celebrating in authentic Parisian style. Thank goodness I have been lucky enough to study and spend every August there for years, just soaking in the magic that is Parisian life.

We transformed an intimate French bistro dining room into an ethereal, glowing, majestic experience straight out of Chateau Versailles, for one night only. Towering silver candelabra, silver trays covered in antique crystal and mercury glass votives were donned with antique crystal bowls (many hand carried by moi back from my favorite Marche de Vanves each summer) filled with floating gardenias, creating a dream of a tablescape. Silver trophies and urns were exploding with hydrangea, parrot tulips, peony, ranunculus, dahlia and soft, feminine blooms while they filled the entire restaurant with the scent of a Parisian perfumerie.

Laduree gift boxes, the birthday girl's favorite Parisian experience, were handpicked and flown in just for the occasion and placed at each guest's seat on top of custom-printed menus detailing the elaborate French seven-course paired tasting meal. Wines from the

host's personal wine cellar were paired alongside dishes covering the gastronomic region from Bordeaux to Epernay.

IMAGINE:

Brown Sugar Roasted Butternut Squash Soup Duck and Garlic Ravioli, Tian of Tarragon Corn Blini, Baby Spinach and Brie Topped with a Pan Roasted Jumbo Diver Scallop, paired with a 2002 Montrachet Grand Cru;

Duo of Big Eye Tuna Thai-Accented Tartar and 5-Spice Seared Loin, Shaved Fennel Salad, Lotus Root Chips, SunnySide up Quail Egg, Foie Gras, Chaud-Froid, Chilled Terrine "Au Torchon" over Rosemary Scented Apple Raisin Chutney and Seared Medallion with Apple Cider Gastrique, paired with 1986 Chateau d Yquem;

Filet of Beef Tenderloin Perigord, Haricot Vert, Truffle Sauce paired with a tasting flight of 1995 Chateau Mouton Rothschild, 1995 Chateau Lafite Rothschild, 1995 Chateau Haut-Brion, 1995 Chateau Latour;

Stylist Secret: Floating Gardenias: Need a fab, fast floral centerpiece for your next party? One of my favorite stylist tricks is to layer silver trays with crystal bowls, filled with water and simple, yet always in classic style floating gardenias. No arranging. No primping. No fuss, no muss. Your entire home is transformed—filled with the glorious scent of everyone's favorite gardenia. Layer in petite votive and tall taper candles—scatter rose petals—and boom. Done.

Roquefort Dressed Baby Field Greens, Crumbled Roquefort Cheese, Toasted Walnuts and Sliced Asian Pear paired with a Strolling Port Cart; and

To finish, Fallen Chocolate Soufflé "Birthday Cake" with a Nut Coated Butterscotch Gelato Truffle served with Dom Perignon Vintage 2000.

I, personally, was on cloud nine with perma-grin fixed for the entire evening. Scratch that—for weeks—just at the thought of the incredible dream of a celebration.

Haute Hostess: Next dinner party, or hey—even wine tasting or cocktail party—design interactive wine/food pairings. Depending on your menu, you can pull your own favorites, that highlight the flavors of each course or small plate. Need a little help? Have your local wine shop do the work for you. Simply share your menu, and they can easily design a pairing that will elevate the tastes of your foods, and create an interactive experience for your guests.

Gougeres

Serves 6

Ingredients:
Pate a Choux (pastry dough)
1/2 cup water
1/2 t. salt
3 tbsp. butter
1/2 cup flour, sifted
2 eggs, beaten
1/2 cup grated Gruyere cheese
freshly ground black pepper
1 egg, beaten
pastry bag, found in grocery aisle, baking supplies
parchment paper

Preparation:
Heat oven to 400°F. In saucepan, over medium to high heat, bring water, salt, sugar, and butter to a boil. Make sure butter is melted. Remove from heat, add in flour, and whip with a wooden spoon until thoroughly mixed. Return to heat on low, and continue whipping until dough forms a solid mass. Remove from heat, and place dough into a mixing bowl. Add in eggs, whipping smooth, until dough forms a smooth consistency. Add cheese and to taste black pepper to pate a choux. Mix thoroughly. Scoop pastry into pastry bag, and pipe out 1" rounds onto parchment paper lined baking sheet. Brush with egg, place in oven, cooking until golden brown, about 20 minutes. Remove, serve warm. Note: these are best prepped, then baked just before guests arrive.

Roquefort Cheese, Toasted Walnuts & Sliced Asian Pear

Serves 6

Ingredients:

1 head leaf lettuce, torn into bite-size pieces
3 pears, chopped
5 oz. Roquefort cheese, crumbled
1 avocado, peeled and diced
1/2 cup thinly sliced green onions
1/2 cup pecans
1/3 cup olive oil
3 tbsp. red wine vinegar

1 t. sugar
1 1/2 t. prepared mustard
1 clove garlic, chopped
fresh ground black pepper to taste

Preparation:

In a skillet over medium heat, toast pecans. Spoon nuts onto a plate. Once cool, break into pieces. For the dressing, blend oil, vinegar, teaspoons sugar, mustard, chopped garlic, salt, and pepper. In a large serving bowl, layer lettuce, pears, blue cheese, avocado, and green onions. Pour dressing over salad, sprinkle with pecans, and dress with fresh black pepper to taste.

A Taste of Tuscany

Dolci

WHEN MY HUSBAND, MIKE, had a big milestone birthday approaching, all he wanted to do was fly to his favorite restaurant in Florence, Italy, for the weekend. He truly wanted to eat his favorite entrée in the entire world for a leisurely, lingering family dinner, drink a few robust Brunello wines and fly home. I confess, my husband's favorite meal in the entire world is lasagna. He craves it weekly. On our honeymoon years ago in Italy, he ate lasagna every single day for lunch and for dinner for an entire week, non-stop. His favorite, meal, ever by far, was the lasagna he had one magical night in the beautiful cellars below Florence, at Buca Mario.

Believe it or not, I thought this plan was ridiculous. But, ahem...I like thoughtful celebrations, so, like any good wife, I humored him. I rang Buca Mario to see if they could help us out—if they would even be open for this nonsense weekend jaunt with a four-

and six-year-old in tow at a fancy Florence restaurant—with full-on jet lag.

Thank heaven, while we were talking about how in the world to fly our family of four, with two small children, to Italy for one crazy night in Florence, my dear friend, Chef Art Smith, insisted he would throw the most authentic Italian birthday party this side of the Atlantic. So, Buca Mario and that irresistible lasagna became the theme for the entire party right here in downtown Chicago.

While Art worked on the menu, I got to work creating the ultimate Tuscan-themed tabletop and party details. Inspired by hand-painted, ceramic Italian vases—we set the color theme. We created a beautiful, masculine palette of camel, chocolate, and green. With textural green lady's slipper and cymbidium orchids, arranged with mini-monstera leaves—we had European style to dress Florentine leather and suede runners, windowsills, bars, buffets, and more. Vintage

Italian glass votives surrounded, evoking the warm ambience of a Tuscan dinner.

Thirty of us were lucky enough to celebrate on the private second floor at Chef Art's restaurant in Chicago, Table 52. It is our favorite romantic spot to toast to a night on the town, and the most beautiful restaurant located in the heart of the city's Gold Coast.

We cocktailed along one side of the warm, intimate, candlelight cathedral ceiling room, sipping prosecco and nibbling on warm passed bites. Next, guests were seated for dinner along the long, elegant European feasting table. It made the cozy room feel much larger than actual size to enjoy cocktailing in one part and dining in another—a great tip to maximize a smaller space. Along with the lush green florals on the tables, each guest had a transporting menu card with a vintage map of Florence and the exact location of Buca Mario as the background.

A few hors d'oeuvres were passed when guests arrived, including Art's famous deviled eggs and drop goat cheese biscuits. Divine! I could eat these two savory tastes for the rest of my entire life, forever and ever.

Chef Art began the meal, with a heartfelt toast to friends, family, and creating beauty around the table. And next, we enjoyed a five-course Tuscan feast that included:

Go Green: We used gorgeous blooms at this party in miniature fluted vases, which is a simple way to design flowers for less. Choose great containers with a small, narrow opening and use just one stem per vase. I like blooms with curved stems, like orchids. It makes designing like a professional effortless, affordable, and easier on the gardens of the world.

Little List: It's easy to throw a party with a personal theme that makes your guest of honor feel special and adored. A little detective work and some creative planning is all you need.

4 Months: Consider what theme you would like to organize your party around. Some ideas include your guest of honor's favorite travel destination, restaurant or meal, favorite color or flower, passion or hobby, dream or goal they've yet to fulfill.

3 Months: Search through old photo albums for inspiration and also for raw material for invitations, menus, and centerpieces. Talk to the loved ones of your guest of honor, like parents, friends, and children to discover what makes them tick, what they dream of, and how they may have been different in the past. All of this is potential material for your party.

2 Months: Decide on your theme and order your nonperishable party elements, unless you are making them yourself (see below): invitations, napkins, menus, CDs, and any other personalized elements you decide to include. (See DIYs #19, #20, #21, #22.)

6 Weeks: Mail invitations.

4 Weeks: Buy any supplies you may need if you are making your own party elements, such as picture frames, vases, napkins, menus and CDs. Complete them over the next two weeks.

Day of: Arrange your customized pieces and celebrate your guest of honor.

wood-fired pizzettes; grilled prawns with polenta; arugula, fennel, and blood orange salad; that famous Buca Mario lasagna, which Chef Art had replicated to an exact science (total miracle, total birthday save by the way), plus Art's famous herbed farmstand focaccia; and dessert. It was all of Mike's favorite foods, and each course was paired with one of his favorite wines. Throughout the night dear friends and family stood, toasted, roasted, and cherished Mike with their words and love. This was a birthday night to remember.

The cake was an exact 3D-replica of the Buca Mario restaurant, baked by the wonderful taste of France a la Chicago, Vanille Patisserie. After Mike blew out the candles,

he stood up and gave a toast of his own to his friends and loved ones. As people finished, they made their way to the chocolate bar, where take-out boxes with custom labels were filled up with chocolate truffles, mini-chocolate-caramel cupcakes, chocolate cookies, and tiered birthday cookies.

And do you know what? Mike now says his favorite lasagna in the world is right here in Chicago...thank you, very much, Chef Art. Who knew that a starry sky of a night in Chicago could feel like fabulous Florence all over again?

Chocolate Truffles
from *Take the Cake*

Ingredients:
Center:
12 oz. milk chocolate, finely chopped
1/3 cup plus 2 tbsp. sweetened condensed milk
1 tbsp. corn syrup

Coating:
1 lb. each: bittersweet chocolate, confectioners' sugar

Preparation:
For the center mixture, place the milk chocolate in a bowl over a saucepan of hot water. Stir to melt the chocolate, about 2 minutes. Remove from heat; stir in the remaining ingredients. (Mixture will become temporarily firm.) Cover; chill 30 minutes. Beat mixture with an electric mixer (with a whisk attachment, if you have one) set on low until the mixture comes together and is

smooth and silky, about 1 minute. (Be careful not to get any water inside.) Scoop small balls of chocolate onto paper-lined pans with a pastry scoop or teaspoon, or use a piping tool with 1/2-inch plain tip to create oval shapes. Freeze about 1 hour. Meanwhile, for the coating, melt the bittersweet chocolate in a bowl over hot water. Sift sugar into a separate bowl. Remove balls from freezer; dip into the melted chocolate, using two forks. Place truffles in the sugar; toss to coat. Let it sit 10 minutes; shake truffles in a strainer to remove excess sugar. Refrigerate in an airtight container. Let come to room temperature before serving.

DIY #11: Trend Forward Table Runner

Create a stunning tabletop with this easy design that uses a runner down the midline of the table. It makes setting your table and designing a centerpiece easier because the eye is drawn to the runner as a focal point.

Decide whether you will use a tablecloth with a runner in a coordinating color, pattern or fabric, or simply a runner on top of a bare table. Both look beautiful, depending on your table. A tablecloth with a runner often creates a more formal look, while a runner alone is more casual (and less expensive). Purchase one runner and tablecloth (if using) per

table. A good rule of thumb is to choose a runner that is either 12–18" longer than your table, so it drapes over the edges, or exactly even with the length of your table. Table runners are widely available in lengths of 70", 90", and 120".

Consider a table runner in a chic print, like Ikat or chevron, raw silk, or simple cotton, depending on the party and the surrounding design. We used a chocolate tablecloth with a camel suede runner at this party.

Layer your runner over the tablecloth or the bare table.

Arrange a floral collection, a candle collection or both down the runner for an instant tabletop. Done!

Birthday Times Two

THE BEAUTIFUL AND BRILLIANT Pam and Bill were celebrating the close of their sensational 60s, with a fabulous, high-energy party that was all about time spent with family and friends. Unlike most birthday parties, these two wanted the spotlight on their loved ones, not themselves.

Both of the birthday guests had big extended families and even more friends. We set the tone for fun from the first impression, with fabulous, colorful invitations, with a memorable detail the couple designed themselves. Each guest's envelope opened to reveal the invitation, with long, flowing ribbons, as a prelude of what was to come at the party. A special, ingenious "Ribbon of Thanks" theme asked guests to think of a source of personal joy or gratitude, which they would write on a ribbon as they arrived at the party, where the ribbons would then be hung from the ceiling as the celebration

unfolded underneath them of life, family and friends, and all things dear.

A gorgeous red theme set the tone for the party, which was held at Chicago's River East Arts Center. Glimmers of gold and splashes of vivid spring green created a colorful energy throughout the space. We backlit tall bar tables with soft, red light, and seating was created from upholstered bar stools for a cocktail feel that was decidedly informal. Gilded glass vases, square votive candles and luscious flowers danced in the red light. We used blooms like orchids, roses, and hydrangeas, peppered with green hypericum berries.

Guests knew it was time to don their dancing shoes, toast double birthday wishes, and celebrate the night away. No one was seated for long and the menu was a smashing array of sizzling small plates, served from roaming food carts throughout the party.

"Shooters" of chilled soups like red beet with crème fraiche, carrot and ginger, and asparagus with a truffled brioche crouton were a perfect spring sip. Guests enjoyed mahi mahi tacos with vegetable slaw, and Kobe sliders with ketchup and onion. The crowd favorite was a spinach salad made with jicama, oranges, and strawberries and topped with poppy seed dressing.

The menu was designed to be eaten on the go, while guests danced to the Ken Arlen Orchestra. The sounds of Motown, disco, and everything in between kept all of the guests happy and shaking it!

Outside, we created an area where guests could cool off and mingle along the river walk overlooking the Chicago River. We set up riverside lounges, sofas, and tables for everyone to enjoy the nighttime spring sky and sip on cocktails from the outdoor bar.

At the final count, three hundred guests danced the night away, enjoying family, friends, and the celebration of two great lives.

Seasonal Savoir-Faire: You don't need lots of space to throw a party during a warm-weather season. Think of the outdoors as an extension of your house. Use an outdoor space for cocktails, then move inside for dinner. You'll instantly multiply your space for entertaining. Just be sure to have an outdoor bar, and outdoor nosh, to help spread the party flow.

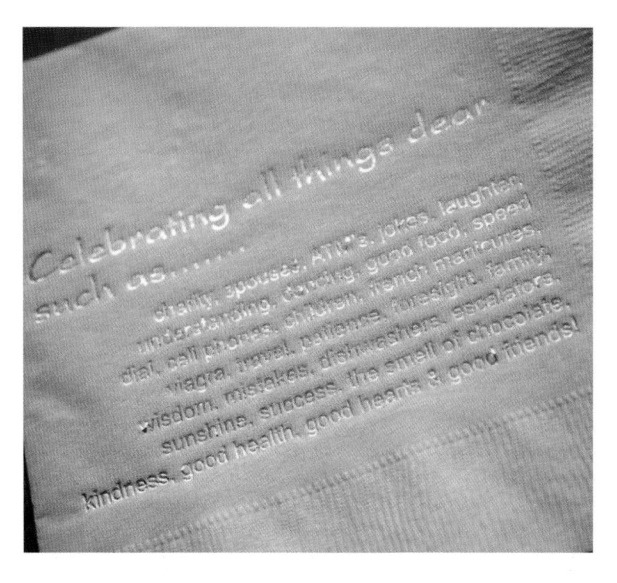

Mahi Mahi Tacos
from J&L Catering
Gluten Free!
Serves 6

Ingredients:
2 lb. mahi mahi filets
1/2 bunch cilantro
3/4 cup red pepper, finely diced
1/2 cup tomatoes, seeded and finely diced
1 jalapeno, finely diced
2 t. coriander
1 tbsp. extra virgin olive oil
1 tbsp. fresh lime juice
Salt and freshly ground black pepper,
to taste
1 avocado, chopped
15 soft corn tortillas

Preparation:
Season mahi mahi filets with salt, pepper and ground coriander. In a pan, sear the fish on both sides. Finish baking in a 350°F oven for 7–10 minutes. In a bowl, break mahi mahi filets into flakes. Add diced red pepper, tomato, jalapeno and chopped cilantro. Add fresh lime juice and olive oil. Warm corn tortillas in skillet until soft. Fill with 1/2 cup of mixture and top with avocado. Serve with salsa.

Lobster Parfaits from J&L Catering
Gluten Free! Serves 6

Ingredients:
1 2-lb. lobster (whole)
1/4 cup fresh lemon juice
1/2 cup fresh chives, chopped
1/2 cup cucumber, finely diced
1/2 cup jicama, finely diced
salt and freshly ground black pepper, to taste
8 martini glasses or other clear glasses

Preparation:
In a large stock pot, bring two quarts of water, with two teaspoons of salt added, to a boil. Once boiling, submerge the lobster and cook for an additional 8–10 minutes. Fill a bowl with cold water and ice cubes while the lobster is cooking, and immediately transfer the lobster to the ice bath when it's done. Once cooled, crack the lobster and pull meat from the shells. Chop lobster meat. In a bowl, mix lobster with lemon juice, chives, and salt and pepper to taste. In martini glasses, alternate layers of lobster mixture and cocktail sauce. Top with diced jicama.

DIY #12: The Gratitude-Ribbon Invitation
We wanted the invitation to get guests excited from the minute it arrived—to celebrate this special couple's theme of "life, family and friends, and all things dear." Follow their lead and send your guests a special, gratitude-ribbon invitation to make an unforgettable impression from the moment they receive it.

Purchase or order your invitations. Choose something that celebrates the occasion and the colors you plan to use. You may want to include some language that explains the gratitude ribbon concept, as we did: "We

are decorating the room with Ribbons of Thanks, which we will tie to lines overhead as we dance and dine. BYO (bring your own) thanks to write on a ribbon as you arrive in celebration of thanks and gratitude."

Purchase coordinating, festive ribbon. You will need three types of ribbon: two thin silk ribbons (1/4–1/2"-wide) for the invitations and one wide silk ribbon (4"-wide) for the gratitude ribbons. Measure how much ribbon you need as follows: For both thin ribbons, double the length of your invitation and purchase enough for each invitation (e.g., if your invitation is 5 inches long, purchase 10 inches of each ribbon per invitation). For the gratitude ribbons, purchase 24–36 inches per invitation, depending on the length of decorative ribbons you desire.

Using a hole puncher, make a hole in the upper left-hand corner of each invitation.

Next, thread through one of each of your thin ribbons, cut to the appropriate length according to your prior measurements. Tie in a simple knot around the corner of the invitation and trim the ends at an angle, allowing the ribbons to dangle decoratively.

Before the party, cut your gratitude ribbons to the desired size, again trimming the ends at an angle.

Display gratitude ribbons with black markers at the entrance to the party, with a reminder for guests to write their messages of thanks.

Once done, hang the gratitude ribbons from clotheslines, mantles, chandeliers…anywhere.

GASOLINE
GAS
FIRE-CHIEF
THIS SALE
$1 0 0
0 8 6
GALLONS
AT
2 8
CENTS PER GALLON
Fire
Chief
With
protective
and detergent
additives
OVER
100
OCTANE

chapter four

CHILDREN'S CELEBRATIONS

WHAT'S A CHILDREN'S PARTY made of? Sugar, spice, everything nice. All it takes is a sprinkling of fun, a dash of imagination and a personalized, kid-centered theme to bring it all together. Remember when one year growing up felt like the equivalent of ten years? Children literally count down to their birthdays and we should too—let's live in, and celebrate the moment along with them. Let's be kids again.

As a mom, I know you're busy. These, kid-friendly ideas are festive, and exciting for the adult guests, too. Planning that next party will be fun, fabulous, and affordable. Celebrations for young ones might be the simplest kind of party planning there is. The guest list all but guarantees the party will be a success...because children love parties!

Come along and learn how to throw a crazy fun party that celebrates all the joys of childhood. After all, childhood goes by too quickly and gatherings of family and friends are cherished memories in the making. And don't forget: great children's parties give you the chance to enjoy being a child again, too, if only for a day.

In this chapter you'll find:

A Cinderella Birthday

WHO DOESN'T WANT to be a princess for a day? A magic castle garden party awaited one very special four-year-old, Quinn. This party was so much fun because it was a little girl's birthday in every way, but thrown with the most grown-up elegance. The driveway had been carpeted in Cinderella-blue carpeting. In the distance, a life-sized Cinderella carriage carried Quinn and Cinderella herself to the gorgeous summertime party. The carriage was royally draped with roses, hydrangeas, and trailing gold ribbons.

At the house, a lush gateway of more flowers, ribbons, and variegated ivory led guests to the backyard, where three tents awaited. Cinderella and the birthday girl greeted the guests as they arrived. Each girl and boy was served a royal goblet of "Princess" or "Prince Punch" and then whisked away to the fairytale land of the costume tent.

Once inside, the children found two racks of royal costumes: one for girls and one for boys.

The girls chose between princess and fairy costumes, and the boys between knight, king, and prince costumes. Then it was off to tent number three, the crafts tent, for some enchanted face-painting and royal tattoos, both beautiful and intricate. The kids completed their outfits with make-your-own tiaras and crowns, using gold paper, markers, toy jewels, and glitter.

Next, the children and parents were led into the royal dining tent, a big, beautiful, oversized "feasting room," where a feast fit for a princess awaited. The children ate miniature favorite, themed foods like, "The Princess and the Pea Salad," star-shaped PB&Js, butterfly-shaped turkey and cheese sandwiches, grilled cheese, "Fairytale Ants on a Log" and "Princess Wands" made of fruit, served, of course, from bartenders and servers in royal garb. Now, of course no royal feast is complete without food and cocktails for the kings, queens, and adults, too, including

lime-mustard grilled summer chicken, truffled egg salad tea sandwiches, and roasted vegetable and goat cheese salad.

In all of the tents, thousands of the perfect Cinderella-blue balloons with long, curly ribbons hovered at the ceiling, creating a whimsical, magical feeling. The tables were long and lovely, with shimmering blue chiffon tablecloths to create a little bling on the tables. Royal "pillows" made of fresh white flowers, with real golden silk tassles and a gilded Cinderella carriage on top, were the centerpieces on the adult tables.

The children's table was all about some serious royal fun. An array of gold revere bowls, pots and julep cups were filled with custom princess pinwheels that appeared to bloom out of wheatgrass. Smaller containers were filled with princess fairy wands and paper noisemakers, all designed to be played with, which made the table as fun as it was beautiful. Sparkly, oversized rings served as napkin rings.

Outside in the backyard, costumed kids were playing on inflatable slides and jumpy castles. Next, Cinderella's carriage came (of course—this is a fairy tale!) and the children had carriage rides and miniature pony rides. Finally, the clock struck 4 o'clock and—alas—like every good tale, the royal ball came to a happy ending.

Go Green: Include dress-up at your next children's party by borrowing costumes from family and friends. Just about everyone with children has them and they can be put to good use, instead of sitting in a closet. Or, get creative with stuff around the house. Mom's inexpensive jewelry becomes princess jewelry, or dad's leather jacket that hasn't fit him since college is perfect for a game of cops 'n robbers. The bottom line? Including costumes is always a hit with kids. Borrowing instead of buying is good for your pocket and good for the environment.

Magical-Shape Sandwiches

from Food for Thought Catering

This simple recipe allows you to create fun and interesting sandwiches, with a unique touch that allows a peek inside the sandwich. Serves 6

Ingredients:
1 loaf whole grain bread
natural peanut butter
low-sugar, all natural jelly
two cookie cutters of your choice,
 one small mini, and one larger

Preparation:
Spread peanut butter on half of your bread slices (not too much now—you have no idea how many kids say to me "this is too peanut buttery. I don't like it"). Do the same with jelly on the remaining slices. Using your smaller cookie cutter, cut out the center of each jelly bread slice (jelly side should be facing up). Discard the centers—or in my house—let the kids feast on these at your side in the kitchen. Next, put peanut butter and jelly pieces together as you would normally, with the jelly piece on top. Take care to avoid pressing too hard, so your cut-out keeps its shape. Using your larger cookie cutter, cut out the prepared sandwiches. Discard crusts and excess bread, or feed it to the kids—or the birds. You're done. Arrange on a plate and serve.

Note: You may substitute or repeat with any ingredients, such as ham and cheddar, turkey and Swiss, and so forth. I recommend choosing healthy bakery fresh natural breads, all natural lunchmeats, and reduced-fat natural cheeses, since these fun, delicious sandwiches are an easy way to get kids the nutrients they need.

The Princess and the Pea Salad

from Food for Thought Catering

Gluten Free! Serves 6

Ingredients:

2 bunches romaine lettuce, rinsed and dried
1 frozen bag petite peas
1/4 lb. aged cheddar cheese, diced into 1/2-inch cubes
2 large hard-boiled eggs, chopped
5 pieces natural turkey bacon, chopped
your favorite balsamic dressing
(my favorite is Garlic Expressions)

Preparation:

Chop the romaine lettuce into bite-sized pieces. Toss chopped romaine with dressing, to lightly coat the leaves. Pour into a serving dish and add peas, cheddar cubes, chopped egg, and chopped bacon evenly over the top.

DIY #13: The Royal Cushion

The perfect centerpiece is just a few flowers away. A royal cushion arrangement works great for children's parties, tea parties, and baby showers alike. All you need are a few inexpensive pieces and you're ready to arrange:

Purchase a square-shaped floral oasis form at your local florist or craft store.

Purchase 4 tassles per oasis from a craft or fabric store.

Purchase 2–3 dozen flowers per oasis. I love inexpensive blooms like carnations. Not only

do they come in a variety of colors, when they're massed together they look really beautiful and rich, even though they're inexpensive. Small spray roses or Daisy Poms also work well, depending on your budget.

The morning of the party, cut your floral oasis so it is not a perfect square by rounding the corners to give it the shape of a pillow.

Fill your sink with clean, warm water. Submerge your oasis upside down and allow it to soak up the water. When it is completely full, it will sink below the surface.

Remove the oasis from the water and set aside.

Trim your flowers so that only about an inch of stem remains.

One at a time, firmly stick the stems into the oasis. The blooms should be snug up against each other, so that none of the oasis is visible. Repeat until you cover it.

Using a pin, fasten a tassel into each corner of the oasis.

Place anything on top of your royal pillow once tabletop to create a final detail. We used a Cinderella carriage, but you could use party store tiaras, crowns, or more.

Gentlemen, Start Your Engines

DAYTONA USA
SEGA
DAYTONA USA
SEGA

A CHILD'S FIRST BIRTHDAY is always one of my favorite celebrations. A little boy named Dylan was turning one! And this day was all about his favorite thing: racecars.

Guests arrived at Dylan's family's home and were beckoned inside by a pathway of colorful car balloons, orange construction cones, and black and white racing pennants. Two fresh-flower "traffic light" topiaries flanked the front door. Round spheres of luscious red roses, yellow daisies, and green orchids said Stop, Yield, Go and kept traffic moving smoothly as guests made their way to the garage, which on this day, would be known only as "the track."

A life-sized racecar made entirely of balloons greeted kids and parents for the perfect photo opportunity. We transformed the garage into a racing playground. A "street" made of black carpet, complete with white

lane markings, ran around the perimeter of the garage. Green Astroturf created the "infield" and hundreds of racing pennants festooned the ceiling. Customized street and road signs peppered the landscape. It was every little boy's dream come true!

Once inside, guests discovered bright, vintage pedal cars for the children to sit in and, with the help of their parents, drive along the street through a series of "pit stops" located at each corner of the garage. The "Car Wash" whisked kids through black-felt washing flaps, complete with big, glossy bubbles and an attendant waxing and shining each car! The "Gas Station" featured a vintage gas pump where kids could fill up their tanks and thirsty parents found a cocktail bar where they could re-fuel, too. The "Body Shop" offered custom car tattoos that celebrated the birthday boy and body painting for the kids.

A long table sat at the heart of the infield. Primary colors of red, yellow, and green, and checkered flags and linens brought the racetrack tabletop. Another road adorned the middle of the table—black and white, with tiny racecars, toy trees, wooden traffic signs and buildings, all to scale. Once again, fun, playable toys made for a very interactive centerpiece. Each child's seat featured a steering-wheel placemat, checkered napkins held in place with a miniature hose-clamp, and orange construction-cone sippy cups.

And the menu? A fantastic buffet of mini-cheeseburgers with checkered racing flags, "Racecar Mac 'n Cheese," "Traffic Light Fruit Kebobs," racecar-shaped PB&Js, chopped Asian salad, and red and white Caprese mozzarella salad.

However, we know that little kids and tables don't work for long, so more toddler fun was to be had outside, pushing racecars through expandable tunnels, racing cars on racecar rugs, and painting their own racecars at the crafts table. Zoom, zoom—we raced to the finish line, for a birthday to remember.

Haute Hostess: At a children's party, it's all about making the tables kid-friendly. This event featured low, children's height dining tables, buffet tables, and kid-sized chairs to really cater to the little ones. We also designed an interactive, take-it-apart centerpiece that worked as decoration and entertainment. Use themed toys and design elements to keep it fun and interesting, and the kids are more likely to stick around, planted in their chairs at the table, for the great menu you've planned.

Mike's Mini Turkey Sliders

Gluten Free! Serves 12

Ingredients:

2 lb. ground turkey
2 oz. Worcestershire sauce
1 container, basil pesto
3/4 cup crumbled feta cheese
1 bunch cilantro, cleaned, trimmed of stems and chopped
freshly ground black pepper, to taste
1 package of 12 whole wheat dinner rolls (can use gluten free, or 6 hamburger buns for large burgers)

Preparation:

Preheat your grill. Mix all burger ingredients in a bowl until just blended. Form 12 small patties. Grill or cook small burgers for 2–3 minutes (regular size burgers for 4–6 minutes on each side) depending on how well-done you like them. Serve burgers on dinner rolls and skewer with a gherkin half (can use toothpick).

Berry Parfaits

Gluten Free!
Serves 6

Ingredients:

1 package fresh raspberries
1 package fresh blueberries

1 package fresh blackberries
1 jar cinnamon
1 jar brown sugar
1 jar cacao powder
1 jar dried lavender
1 jar dried orange peel
1 large container vanilla yogurt
(I love Stonyfield Farms)
1 large container lemon yogurt
1 large container chocolate yogurt
12 parfait glasses
(Stylist Secret: I love cordial glasses)

Preparation:
Wash and pat dry all berries. Place berries in glasses.

Place toppings, sprinkles, and yogurts into small bowls or glasses with spoons for guests to self serve.

DIY #14: Photo-Op Favors
Everyone loves a memento, a take away, a party favor. What better way to greet your guests than with a special photo-op and a treasured picture they take home? You don't have to stage anything elaborate... or...maybe you do. A simple reminder of the party is all that's needed:

Make sure you have a Polaroid or Digital camera with printer on hand, since you want to send your guests home with the special picture. (Maybe a friend or family member has one for you to borrow.) Count your number of young guests and buy the necessary amount of film. Secret tip: I double the

number of film needed, to account for two for each young guest.

Create a simple, memorable photo frame by choosing cardstock or another heavier-weight paper (even construction paper works) in a color that matches your palette. Decorate the paper with stamps, stickers, or other embellishments that carry on your party theme. (This is a great activity to include your child in. Family craft time = fun time.)

Cut to size, usually 4" x 8".

Fold the pieces of paper in half and—voilà!—your perfect frame is complete.

At the party, use a small piece of double-sided tape to attach each guest's photo to the inside of the frame.

Of course, think of your creative photo-op! Maybe you're throwing a fiesta and a giant piñata is the vocal point. Or maybe your home or backyard has a gorgeous setting that could provide the backdrop. Let your imagination run wild, and don't forget to ask your child for his or her ideas.

Girly Pedi Party

EVERY LITTLE GIRL DREAMS of the day she'll become a grown-up. So we created the ultimate Fancy Nancy spa party for Elizabeth's 10th birthday. She and her friends were treated to an afternoon of pampering that was pretty in pink plus a whole lot more. We set the tone with fun nail polish bottle invitations, with a 3D-handle that popped right out of the top.

Elizabeth loves hot pink, so pink for the day it was. Hot pink linens, utensils, food, and drink help set the scene for an afternoon of pampering and celebration.

Each girl was greeted with cup of pink "Sparkly Spa Juice." Matching straws and napkins created an inviting look. The sounds of Wicked and High School Musical could be heard in the background. Cool music playlists are a must do for a successful tween-age party.

We brought in an experienced spa team from Chicago's Beauty on Call to give the girls the royal treatment. Four stations were a fantastic whirlwind of spa specialties, which the girls popped around to visit one at a time. Mini-manis were followed by mini-pedis. Then it on to red carpet up-dos and a sparkly make-up station.

This event works best with a smaller number of guests for personal and attention at every step, which can be more difficult with a larger group.

The menu for the party was—you guessed it, all pink! On a long, pink-dressed buffet table, we had all kinds of fun sweet and savory snacks. Because the party was in the middle of the afternoon, we didn't have to serve a full meal. Great party planning secret: if you don't want to serve a full menu, choose a time that's between mealtimes and save yourself the extra preparation.

Delicious "Spa Snacks," created from a salty and sweet trail mix, were served in waffle cones—right from the grocery aisle. We also had a variety of pink candies, in celebration of all-things-sweet. Childhood favorite pink sugar wafer cookies, meringues, and more were housed in different glass trifle bowls and vintage containers for a lovely, varied look. Candy scoops were provided and used to fill pink takeout boxes with each girl's favorite treats (though spoons work beautifully, too.)

For the spa-themed birthday cupcake, we arranged pink-frosted cupcakes on a tiered cake stand for an effortlessly elegant look. Miniature nail polishes and lipsticks were nestled on top of the frosting for custom finish.

Soon, we lit the candles on the cupcakes and sang "Happy Birthday" and the girls departed, as graceful and glamorous as little ladies after being pampered like grown-ups for the afternoon.

Seasonal Savoir-Faire: In the winter, when you can't be outside in your backyard, it's nice to have a smaller party indoors (8–10 guests). Pick a theme that allows you to have an intimate group and take advantage of the coziness to really honor your guests. Some great ideas for winter children's parties include: a make-your-own grilled pizza party, Cupcake Wars party, or Messterpiece Madness, where the kids make art projects and crafts.

Little List: Make your child part of the party-planning process and include his or her ideas on the big day. Involving your child helps teach them at an early age how to celebrate and spend time with friends and family. Much too often, we adults try to choose what we want to do—but then we aren't being inclusive, sharing and teaching the true beauty of personalized celebrations alongside the child.

2–3 Months: Start asking your child about what he or she would like to do for a birthday party this year. Sit down together and explain how he or she can choose the theme and help create the details for the party. (You can't believe the ideas kids come up with—ones the parent never would have thought of!) Here, we did a spa theme, with a pink candy bar, and cupcakes with hot pink frosting with a toy lipstick or tube of nail polish on top. You could do your child's favorite with linens and desserts to match, and then add a unique touch like this. (See DIY #17.)

2 Months: Order the invitations if you're getting them professionally done or start making them if doing by hand.

6 Weeks: Plan your menu together. What kinds of foods does your child like? Come up with fun variations that work with your theme.

1 Month: Mail invitations.

2 Weeks: Make decorative elements for your party. Again, follow your child's lead, but with your guidance! (See DIY #18.)

1 Week: Shop for nonperishable menu items.

2 Days: Shop for remaining fresh menu items.

1 Day: Decorate the house or party location and prepare most of your menu. Do prep work for items that need to be fixed tomorrow. Make sure to involve your child in the mix of the getting ready, whether it's emptying candy into bowls, arranging cookies on a platter, or helping you make sandwiches. This will help them feel like it's really their party.

Day of: Happy Birthday!

Sparkly Spa Juice

The beautiful, bright pink color of this drink, in all of its fizzy goodness, begs for clear glasses or cups. I also recommend colored straws to complete the look.

Serves 6

Ingredients:

16 oz. all natural pomegranate-cranberry juice
8 oz. lemon flavored sparkling water
lemon juice
raw sugar
organic raspberries

Preparation:

Before the party, pour lemon juice into a shallow dish. Pour sugar into a separate shallow dish. Turn glasses upside down, and dip each glass into the juice, shaking off excess. Dip same glass rim into the bowl of sugar. Combine juice and soda in a pitcher of your choice. Fill each sugar-rimmed glass with plenty of ice cubes and pour. Drop in a few berries and serve with a straw.

Spa Snacks

Ingredients:

2 cups caramel popcorn
2 cups cheese popcorn
1 cup mini-pretzels
1/4 cup dried cranberries
1/4 cup golden raisins
1/4 cup yogurt-covered raisins
1/4 pink candies, such as M&Ms

Preparation:

Combine ingredients in a bowl. Toss several times to marry flavors together. Serve in paper cones (see DIY #18), waffle cones, glass bowls with scoops, individual glasses or tea cups, cellophane bags sealed with a custom stamped label, or paper favor bags.

DIY #15: The Cupcake Cake

Make dessert something to remember with this easy, memorable presentation:

Purchase from a bakery, or bake your own cupcakes. Be sure to choose a frosting color that

accentuates the theme of your party. (If making your own, a few drops of food coloring does the trick.)

Purchase an equal number of decorations for your cupcakes, like the tiny lipstick and nail polish containers we used. Craft stores and dollar stores are usually brimming with creative objects to complement your party's theme or stir the imagination.

Place your fun theme-pieces on top of your cupcakes. The frosting will act like glue.

Arrange cupcakes on a tiered cake stand. (Easy instant cake stand: turn bowl upside down, place plate on top, using floral cling or museum tack to "stick" them together.) All done. The colored frosting and extra detail makes your cupcakes look wonderful, expensive, and unique.

DIY #16: Snack Cones

Snacks are easy to display in waffle cones, or if you prefer, colorful paper cones.

Using scissors, cut your cardstock into squares so your cones are kid-sized.

Decorate each piece of cardstock.

One piece at a time, curl a corner in towards the center of the page. Continue curling paper into the shape of a cone, so that the curled corner is tight and pointy at the bottom, and the top is open.

Secure the edge of the cone with glue or double-sided tape.

Fill and display in individual glasses or a basket.

Asian Tea Shower Menu
in honour of
Mychelle
Peking Duck, Sliced Green Onions and Plum
in a Petite Tied Lettuce Wrap
Crab, Cream Cheese and Cucumber
Smoked Salmon Wasabi Tea
Sesame Lo Mein
Carrot, Cucumber, Jicama,
Tossed in a Sesame Oil
Ginger Scones

chapter five

SHOWERED WITH LOVE

A SHOWER IS A MAGICAL EVENT that celebrates a new beginning. From bridal showers to baby showers, we join together to mark a new chapter in the guest of honor's life. I think because of this, showers are especially easy, joyful, inspired events to host. There is already so much love in the air—anticipation for the big day ahead, whatever it may be—that the party itself is a bit of a breeze.

In this chapter you'll find:

- *Hey Baby—Couples 'n Cocktails*
- *Blue Willow Bridal Tea*
- *Spring's New Arrival*

Many showers are thrown with a group of friends, which further divvies up the responsibility. I think the best showers happen when each person takes charge of one piece of the planning that inspires them, whether it's invitations, favors, the menu or executing the set-up the day of the shower. This way, the workload is spread across several people, and each can focus on his or her passion, or favorite entertaining element.

Whether you're planning a shower alone or as part of a group, for a mom-to-be or a bride-to-be, the fundamentals are the same: personalized details, a wonderful menu, fun activity, and warm, charming hosts.

Hey Baby—Couples 'n Cocktails

B

COUPLES SHOWERS *aren't* just for weddings. We gathered Laura and Jim's closest friends, to celebrate the happy, joyful occasion of the birth of their first child. Rather than the typical lunch shower, cocktails and hors d'oeuvres were on the menu. It is a fun twist on tradition to buck the more expected shower trend and host an elegant evening cocktail soiree for both mom and dad to celebrate in style.

A beautiful antique baby carriage stood in the entry, centered on top of the foyer table, welcoming guests as they arrived. We filled the precious wicker buggy with a colorful mix of seasonal fresh flowers, including magenta tulips, cream roses, and pale green hydrangea. It was a beautiful way to set the tone as guests arrived, with the pretty, petite details guests would be enchanted with throughout the evening.

As soon as guests walked through the door, they were served chilled "Baby-tinis," made of organic vodka and cherry-lime juice. We served it in old-fashioned glass baby bottles, with straws for easy sipping. Always, always at baby showers, we had an alcohol-free "mock-tail" ready and waiting for Laura, so she could enjoy the "same" cocktail with the best of them. Like a first impression cocktail always does, the "Baby-tini" was festive, delicious, and created a conversation piece from the moment guests arrived.

We celebrated the upcoming arrival with a variety of baby-sized foods, which were served on vintage wooden children's puzzles and colorful laminated placemats, bought especially for the occasion. All of the dishes were done in one-bite servings, which meant the guests did not need silverware or to be seated to enjoy eating them, keeping the atmosphere light and casual, and the square footage and party preparation to a minimum.

The whimsical nibbles included macaroni and cheese bites on spoons, and spaghetti and meatball bites, served on forks. The guests also enjoyed baby crab-cakes with dollops of wasabi cream; baby cheeseburgers, with truffled frites; and mini-curry–chicken sandwiches, made on fresh bakery breadsticks, our stylist secret: miniature version of baguettes.

Tomato goat cheese soup sips were served in tiny glass baby bottles, with a jumbo shrimp cocktail perched on top Parties are all about presentation, and using themed props for serving trays, platters, food vessels and more really injects personal style and the theme into the party details.

Soon, we gathered everyone in the dining room for the group activity—a given at every shower event. "A Baby-Food Tasting" game was custom designed to be enjoyed and tasted by each adult—at a sit down dining table. The table was beautifully decorated with flowers, candles, and formal china. At each place setting, guests found an adorable collection of five baby foods, with custom labels that were numbered for a true taste-testing. Each couple was asked to sample and guess the flavors, using baby spoons and all. The first couple to guess all five correctly was the big winner.

After the game, dessert was served. A beautiful cake in the shape of a baby block, had the letters B-A-B-Y written across the side in fondant. A variety of "baby" bite size desserts reminded guests of their own childhood favorites, including miniature éclairs, meringues, macaroons, cupcakes, and whoopee pies. Everyone loves to feel young again, and what better reason to celebrate than the arrival of a brand new baby.

Little List: Take adult comfort foods and transform them into baby-size pieces for a creative twist on the typical baby shower. It's fun to find tiny bite-size hors d'oeuvres and favorite comfort-food entrees that you can transform into smaller, "baby" foods for adults. Serve the bites on children's puzzles and colorful laminated placemats to remind everyone that a baby is on the way.

2 Months: Plan your menu of comfort foods. Think of past and present favorites, and any current cravings for the mom-to-be, like: macaroni and cheese, spaghetti and meatballs, grilled cheese, burgers, mini quarter-cut sandwiches, soups and more. Visit your local grocery or gourmet market to determine what items they have in stock or on a catering menu. Decide what you will prepare yourself and what you will order pre-made, like we did. If time is of the essence, order everything. Stylist secret: Do not feel you need to make your menu from scratch.

1 Month: Count out your silverware to determine what you may need to buy or borrow. Remember, you can skewer many foods onto forks or serving bites on spoons. Plan on two bites of each food per guest for heavy hors d'oeuvres.

3 Weeks: Count out your serving trays. One per type of food should do it. Decide whether you will use children's puzzles, books, laminated children's placemats or all three. Purchase puzzles, books, placemat materials, and make your designs. (See DIY #31.)

2 Weeks: Finalize your guest count and place your order for pre-made food items.

3 Days: Buy your groceries for the remainder of your menu.

1 Day: Prepare all menu items that can be made ahead of time. Prep ingredients for items that will be made tomorrow.

Day of: Finish cooking your foods and pick-up pre-made items. Assemble your dishes onto forks and spoons, about a medium-sized bite per utensil. Serve on children's puzzles and/or laminated placemat trays. For larger parties, you can keep extra fork- and spoonfuls in the kitchen and replenish serving trays throughout the party.

Spaghetti n' Meatballs en "Fork"

Gluten Free option!

Serves 6

Ingredients:

1 box Penne Pasta (can use gluten free)
2 jars gourmet Arabiatta (spicy red) Sauce
2 lb. ground turkey
1 lb. spicy Italian sausage, casings removed
3/4 cup cracker crumbs (can use gluten free)
1/4 cup parsley flakes
1 egg, beaten
1/2 tsp. garlic powder
1 small onion, minced
1/3 cup ketchup
fresh ground pepper

Preparation:

Combine beef and sausage. Add in remainder of ingredients and mix together well with hands. Heat oven to 350°F. Form meat mixture into quarter size balls, and place on baking sheet. Bake in oven for 10 minutes, per side, flipping meatballs over so browned on each side. When cooked, add 1 jar sauce and keep warm. Cook pasta in boiling water, per package directions. Toss in pasta sauce till well coated. To serve, place two penne on the end of a fork, then add small meatball. Line a serving tray with forks and garnish with fresh pepper.

Tomato Soup Sips with Gulf Shrimp
Gluten Free!
Serves 6

Ingredients:
4 oz. fresh goat cheese, crumbled
2 lb. tomatoes, chopped
1 tbsp. olive oil
2 medium onions, chopped
2 cloves garlic, chopped
1/4 cup fresh basil, chopped
4 cups chicken broth
freshly ground pepper
springs of fresh basil for garnish
1 package fresh or frozen peeled, deveined cooked shrimp, tail on

Preparation:
Set shrimp out to thaw, if frozen. Follow directions on package. In a large soup pot, heat oil over low heat. Add the onions and garlic; cook 8 minutes, stirring often. Add 2/3 the basil, pepper and the tomatoes and cook, stirring for 10 minutes. Raise the heat to high, add chicken broth and bring to a boil. Reduce the heat to low, partially cover and let simmer for 20 minutes. Remove the soup from heat and add goat cheese, stirring well to make sure that all the cheese is incorporated. Let cool. Working in batches, puree the soup in a food processor or blender until smooth. Taste for seasoning and add pepper as needed. If the soup has an acidic taste, add a pinch of sugar. To serve hot, bring the soup to a simmer for about 5 minutes. Pour with ladle into small glass baby bottles, shot glasses or small cordials. Top with chopped basil for garnish. Place shrimp on cutting board, and garnish with fresh black pepper. Place one shrimp in each soup sip, with the tail hanging over the rim as a "handle."

Blue Willow Bridal Tea

Asian Tea Shower Menu
in honour of
Mychelle
Peking Duck, Sliced Green Onions and Plum
in a Petite Tied Lettuce Wrap
Crab, Cream Cheese and Cucumber
Smoked Salmon Wasabi Tea
Sesame Lo Mein
Carrot, Cucumber, Jicama
Tossed in a Sesame Oil
Ginger Scones

A GORGEOUS ASIAN TEA bridal shower was thrown in hues of pink, blue and cream. The inspiration on this day? The bride-to-be's family heirloom collection of blue willow china. From the invitations to the luncheon serving pieces, all of the shower details were inspired by the family's elegant, heirloom china pattern.

The bride and her mother had a wonderful collection of cake stands, plates, and teacups inherited from a long line of relatives, which we used with stunning Asian-inspired flowers. Creamy and pink cymbidium orchids were clipped short and tucked into pink and white glass vases. A beautiful menu was designed on pink cardstock, and printed in the perfect shade of blue willow ink, with a matching knotted ribbon for the perfect finishing touch.

Before feasting on a series of delicious Asian fare, the guests cocktailed outside on the gorgeous garden patio. Paper lanterns

hung from the trees and cocktail tables were draped with shimmering white fabric, and topped with Asian inspired ceramic containers of floating gardenias and votives.

A refreshing "Mandarin Orange Tea-ni" was the specialty cocktail, made with freshly brewed white tea, mandarin orange juice and orange vodka. After a bit of sipping and a lot of catching up, the ladies moved inside for an elegant, sit-down lunch. The tables were adorned with the cream and pink Cymbidium Orchids, with the beautiful menus tucked into linen napkins, finished with a pocket fold. The bride herself—fabulously clever as she is—made the custom blue willow linens for the luncheon.

We created unique warmth by placing votive candles in sake cups, which were an inexpensive, but beautiful, touch for this Asian-inspired affair, combining the more traditional flair with a

more modern appeal. Bamboo folding chairs for each dining chair completed our Asian theme.

Rows of tiered blue willow china cake stands were set all the way down the center of the long, linear table. Guests helped themselves to teriyaki-marinated shrimp wrapped in snow peas, spring rolls with chili-coriander dipping sauce, smoked salmon with wasabi cream cheese tea sandwiches, and sesame lo mein salad.

After lunch, everyone moved into the family room for dessert and opening gifts. Hot tea was served with ginger scones with clotted cream and jams, chocolate-dipped fortune cookies with custom bridal messages inside, almond cookies and mango sorbet topped with fresh lime zest.

Guests picked up a festive pink favor as they departed. Frosted-pink takeout boxes were wrapped with bright pink ribbon and two sets of decorative chopsticks, and filled with collections of Asian teas inside. It was the perfect ending and keepsake for the guests to enjoy all summer, remembering an afternoon spent toasting together in lovely Lincoln Park.

Haute Hostess: My dad is the most amazing chef—everyone loves it when he's in the kitchen. He's famous for zesting fresh citrus over his ice cream or sorbet, just as we did at this shower. This unbelievably easy stylist secret changes the flavor of everyday ice cream to be otherworldly—fresh and delicious. The next time you're serving dessert, simply use a zester to grate lime over mango sorbet, lemon over vanilla ice cream, or any combination you crave. It takes only a few seconds and is an easy way to instantly dress up dessert.

Shrimp in Snow Peas

from George Jewell Catering

Gluten Free!

Serves 6

Ingredients:

1 large green cabbage, sliced in half through the center to create two halves

1 tbsp. peanut oil

1 lb. fresh or frozen raw shrimp, peeled, deveined and tails removed

1 bottle, all natural ginger sesame dressing marinade

1 bunch fresh dill

1/2 lb. fresh snow peas

freshly ground black pepper

Go Green: Using heirloom tablewares at a shower adds a sentimental touch to a family gathering. We celebrated the bride-to-be's family at this shower, and their collection of willow blue china, by choosing favorite pieces from the bride's mom, aunts, and even some pieces that were inherited from her grandmother. In this case, using family pieces instead of renting or buying new ones also added a personal touch to the shower.

Preparation:

If shrimp are frozen, thaw according to packaging. Toss in ginger sesame dressing, and marinate for an hour. Place oil in skilled, sauté shrimp until pink. Remove shrimp from skillet. Trim snow pea ends. Bring water to boil in stockpot. Prepare an ice water bath, in a second stockpot. Add snow peas to boiling water, and boil for 2 minutes. Wrap snow pea around each shrimp, securing with small skewer.

Stylist Secret: Place cabbage half, flat side down, onto platter or cutting board. Insert skewers into cabbage to stand on end for a dramatic presentation.

Spring's New Arrival

SOMETIMES, THE SMALLEST PARTIES can be the most enjoyable. I love an intimate party with fewer guests, which means you can celebrate in style and with a highly personalized touch. On this day, a wonderful group of a dozen women (and one token male!) gathered for the most intimate and elegant spring baby shower to celebrate the birth of a dear friend's very first child.

We chose a bright and feminine green and pink color theme for the shower. Silver julep cups, stemware, and florals in sweet pinks, whites and greens dressed the tables. At each place, guests found a hand-calligraphied placecard, "planted" in a silver julep cup and brimming with moss. Each julep cup was set atop a crisp white napkin and clear glass charger plate, with silver detail at the edges.

All of the glasses on the tables were decorated with pink- and blue-colored sugar at the rims—a nod to the playful baby shower.

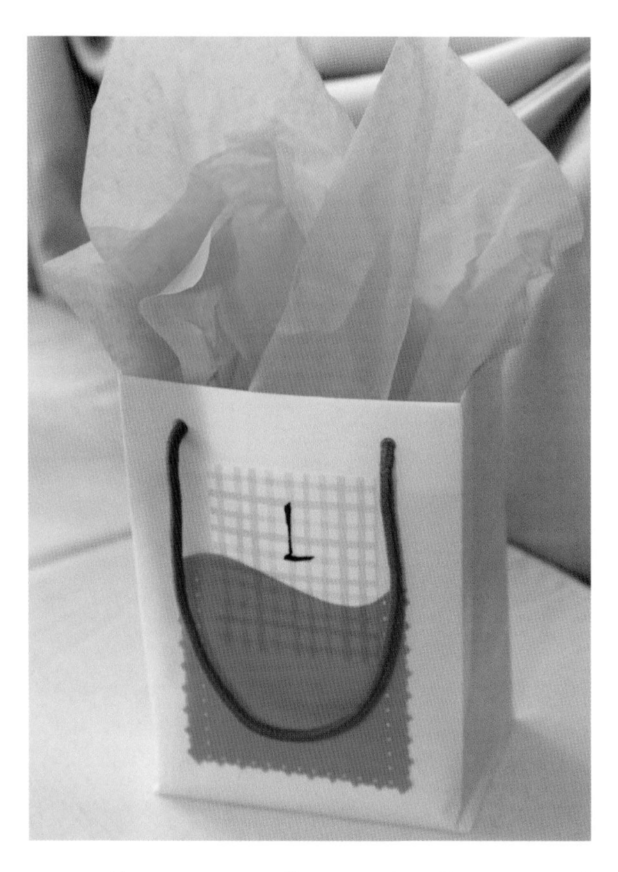

Simply dip each glass in a shallow bowl of lemon juice, shake off the excess, then into a shallow bowl of colored sugar, for a stylized glass for each guest.

Even the chairs had a fresh, springtime look. We dressed traditional white wooden chivari chairs with hand dyed pink and green silk ribbon, woven into the bamboo slats. At each seat was an adorable favor, a collection of chic pamper yourself, bath and body lotions, aromatherapy candles and other sweet treats, inside glossy white gift bags with custom tags tucked in with the first initial of every guest's name.

The lunch was served buffet-style, with a fresh, springtime tabletop for guests to sit and enjoy each other's company. A sumptuous buffet of petite tea sandwiches; roasted beet salad with goat cheese and apples; and minted fruit skewers served with sesame

soba noodle salad in mini-takeout boxes. Stylist secret: glossy garden fresh lemon leaves surrounded the vintage silver trays for texture and detail.

A guest book for baby was the special focus for the afternoon. Each guest signed in as she arrived and wrote a special message to new mother and her soon-to-arrive baby—of course the most special guests of the day. Later, the book was completed with a copy of the invitation, printed menu and all of these gorgeous photographs. Even guests who weren't able to make the shower were there in spirit. They sent cards and special messages to be included in the book, allowing Lisa to read and to savor, as she enjoyed an afternoon with her closest friends and family, both near and far.

Seasonal Savoir-Faire: A baby shower is the perfect opportunity to use all fresh, local fare. Choose organic, natural ingredients to cater to the healthy new mom. These farm-to-table foods are the freshest and also have the most flavor, in addition to reducing the amount of pesticides and other chemicals that the mom-to-be and her baby are exposed to. Visit local farmers' markets or the grocery produce aisle to make shopping fun, farm fresh, and "green."

Fruit Lollipops with Mint and Honey
Gluten Free! Serves 6

Ingredients:
1/2 lb. honeydew
1/2 lb. cantaloupe
1/2 lb. pineapple
1/2 lb. strawberries
honey
freshly chopped mint
12 wooden skewers

Preparation:
Wash fruit and chop into 2" pieces. (Shortcut: Buy pre-cut fruit at the grocery store to save a step). Toss fruit pieces with fresh chopped mint until just blended. Place fruit on skewers, alternating the type of fruit with each piece. Arrange skewers on a platter and drizzle with honey.

Stylist tip: Place a maximum 3 pieces of fruit on each skewer, so they are easy to pop in your mouth gracefully.

Roasted Beets with Goat Cheese and Apples
Gluten Free! Serves 6

Ingredients:
Salad:
1 lb. red beets, washed with ends trimmed
2 tbsp. olive oil
1 lb. mesclun greens, rinsed and dried
2 apples
5 ounce pasteurized goat cheese
(make sure it is pasteurized if serving to anyone who is pregnant!)

Dressing:
1/3 cup orange juice, freshly squeezed if possible
3 tbsp. olive oil
2 tbsp. balsamic vinegar

1 tbsp. Dijon mustard
2 t. honey
salt and freshly ground black pepper to taste

Preparation:
Preheat oven to 350°F. Wash the beets thoroughly, leaving skins on, removing green leaves. Place beets in a roasting pan, and toss with 2 tablespoons of olive oil. Cover, and bake for an hour, until a knife can slide easily through the largest beet. Set aside, or keep in the refrigerator overnight if preparing in advance. Core and chop your apples into small pieces. In a medium-sized bowl, combine mesclun greens, beets, and apples. In a separate bowl, whisk dressing ingredients together. Toss with salad until just coated. Crumble goat cheese over the top. Grind with fresh black pepper.

DIY #17: Ribbon Treatment for Chairs
Ribbon is a simple way to dress up any chair with a slatted back, and embellish your party's color theme in the process.

Purchase two 36" pieces of double-faced satin ribbon (1 1/2-2" wide) per chair.

Weave one piece of ribbon through the slats, whether vertical or horizontal, and tie in a bow or knot around one side of the chair.

Weave the second piece of ribbon in the other direction, so you finish with a bow or knot on the other side of the chair.

Repeat for all chairs.

Trim the edges at an angle for a uniform ribbon length on all chairs. (Stylist secret: Never, ever leave straight edges on the ends of a ribbon!)

DIY #18: Baby Advice for Mom Book
The guest book we made at this shower achieved three goals in one: it captured the

details of the special day, provided a fun shower activity for guests to participate in, and created a cherished keepsake for mom and baby to enjoy always, even including the messages of guests who weren't able to attend. This guest book is an easy and touching inclusion for any type of baby shower and a great replacement for a traditional goofy game.

Purchase a scrapbook or photo album with blank pages that also coordinates with your baby shower theme.

Contact out-of-town guests or other guests who can't attend the shower and ask them to send a card, letter, or other special message for the baby. Even an email works.

Glue the shower invitation onto the first page of the album.

Glue the menu onto the second page of the album.

Glue the out-of-town guests' messages onto separate pages, for mom to read at the shower.

The day of the shower, make sure you have pretty pens for guests to sign in as they arrive.

During the shower, pass around the book and ask each guest to write advice to the new mom, or thoughts for the new baby. This can be everything from a fun story about the mom-to-be, a piece of advice, an expression of love...anything.

After the shower, complete the album with pictures from the party and give it to the guest of honor.

chapter six

BEFORE THE WEDDING

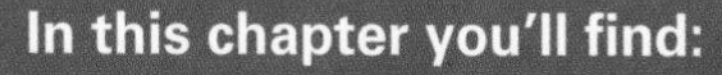
In this chapter you'll find:

- *Engagement Cocktails*
- *"I Do" Dinner*
- *Lilly Pulitzer Tea Party*
- *Cypress Sunset Soirée*
- *Dinner on the Lake*

I MAY LOVE nothing more than a wedding.

Weddings celebrate the love of our life—in the warm circle of our closest friends and family. And that moment in time, that group of our favorite people in the entire world, traveling from near and far, are only together once in our lifetime. Amazing. Sacred.

The wedding parties begin moment one upon an engagement. There is so much to celebrate—so much love in the air.

With elegant engagement parties, showers and rehearsal dinners, many brides and grooms may feel as if they're married before the "I Dos" have been exchanged and the marriage certificate has even been requested. One thing's for certain: when caught in the midst of planning that very special wedding day, pre-wedding celebrations offer carefree enjoyment for the bride, the groom, and the bridal parties alike.

Parties before the wedding are enjoyable dress rehearsals, whether in name or in spirit. It's easy to get the nuptial vibes going with a small, simple engagement party for family and friends, or with a grand rehearsal dinner. Whatever the case, celebrating the months and days that lead up to a wedding are a chance for the bride and groom to sit back and enjoy the magic of this unforgettable time in their lives.

Engagement Cocktails

"We're engaged!" Guests gathered for an engagement party that was inspired by his and hers Great Tastes...farmers' market cocktails, global cuisine, and all things sweet. I love this theme, this pretty, elevated tasting meal, and the high energy level it brings to parties. So, to celebrate the newly engaged, skip the predictable daytime ladies luncheon menu and create an elegant, delicious experience of tasting favorite foods, especially the bride and groom's.

A farm-to-table fresh picked produce Married Muddling Bar was on display to entice guests as they arrived. Each glass was filled with guests' choice of colorful fresh fruit muddled, spirits and mixers hand chosen, mixed inside, and served with a smile.

Every party detail brimmed with a fresh spring palette. French-inspired arrangements of tulips, sweetpea, roses, and orchids were designed in crystal and vintage silver vases,

surrounded by flickering candlelight.

The easy buffet-style menu was delectable, and arranged before guests arrived.

Many of the items were pre-made, so all we had to do was arrange them on plates before guests arrived, perfect for a simple, affordable and gourmet party.

We served a taste of Italy, on top of modern tasting plates, with salumi, pecorino, and darling petite fig chutney spoons. A sinfully savory Korean BBQ taco stand was the big hit, creating yet another interactive build-your-own tasting experience. Guests absolutely love to see and taste new things at parties—and this was a visual feast. Caesar Salads were served in tiny, bite size "cups," Shrimp Rolls made for a pretty bite of spring, BBQ Duck, and Beet Napoleons, and Indian Fusion small plates with Tandoori Chicken,

Veg Samosas, and Yogurt Raita with Naan rounded out the major menu fun.

We made sure to include some sweet treats, too, since the groom was a chocolate lover. An acrylic "cocktail cupcake" tower was the stunning centerpiece to the petite sweets bar, designed in mini "more-sel" size with aplomb by More Cupcakes. Mojito Cakes, Gin and Tonic Cakes, Margarita Cakes, and more traditional flavors filled each tier.

In between mouthfuls, guests hugged and congratulated the happy couple and took Polaroid pictures, which were signed with sweet congratulatory messages and kept in an album as a memento of the day.

Married Mudding Bar

Ingredients:
Sprits: Vodka, Gin, Rum
Mixers: Club Soda, Sparkling Water, Tonic, Simple Syrup
Fresh Fruit: cubed Watermelon, Blueberries, Black Berries, Strawberries, Raspberries, Mango, Pineapple
Fresh Herbs: Mint, Rosemary, Thyme

Preparation:
Pull together a collection of mixed size glass containers (you want to see the colors coming through—it creates a gorgeous focal point on the bar and a dramatic first impression) and fill each container with fruit and herbs. Guests will walk up, pick a glass, choose their ingredients, and choose their spirit and mixers. Guests can self serve, or

Haute Hostess: When you're celebrating a couple, it's a nice touch to use their wedding date, monogram, photographs or any other personalized detail at the party. Decorate cupcakes and cookies with icing and monogram the happy couple's initials as an easy, thoughtful touch.

a bartender can assist for smooth service, muddling fruit and herbs in the glass, then adding ice, liquor and mixers. Garnish with fresh herbs or a skewer of fresh fruit. (Stylist tip: Edible flowers are a beautiful garnish as well. I love to use Pansies).

Italian Trio Tasting Plate

Ingredients:
pecorino cheese
truffle honey (can also puree honey and truffle paste in blender)
rosette de Lyon salami
fig chutney (or jam)

Preparation:
Use small plates (we used a disposable clear plastic plate here, with three sepa rate sections, but have also done this as a "triangle" on a round small cocktail plate). You can use almost anything, but the sections make each stand out. We also used a tiny tasting spoon, often used to sample ice cream. Demitasse spoons for espresso are also the perfect size. Slice Pecorino into triangular wedges and place one on each plate. Drizzle with truffle honey. Slice salami super thin (this can be done at counter when purchasing) and fold twice. This gives the slice some depth and makes it "bloom" on the plate. Place on the plate next to the pecorino. Finally, place small amount of chutney on a tiny spoon and add to the plate. It's meant to be eaten in the order of assembly, as the last component, the fig chutney, is an Italian palate cleanser.

“I Do” Dinner

PEACH
SALSA
SHANIA AND DEMOND'S
WEDDING WEEKEND
Emergency Kit

SOMETIMES, WE ARE LUCKY ENOUGH to be transported as we celebrate, to a setting so exquisite, so serene, so plucked from a feature film, that we have to pinch ourselves that this is real, and that the party is really unfolding right in front of our eyes. Our "I Do" Dinner was a family affair, merging two separate families from different parts of the country together, into one heck of a giant, southern style backyard barbeque party.

The eighteenth hole at the Inn at Palmetto Bluff was out backdrop for the evening, and as the sunset, the setting was lit with a blazing orange, firey painted sky.

We welcomed guests to the weekend wedding celebration with silkscreened jute tote bags, filled to the brim with everything one could need seaside for the weekend—including French lavender bug spray, monogrammed his and hers emergency first aid kits, custom

crosswords and puzzles, southern savory treats like sweet spiced pecans, peach salsa, fresh fruits, weekend itineraries, maps, and more.

Upon arrival at dinner, glowing lanterns created illuminated pathways through the golf course, on walkways, terraces, around the firepit—everywhere you turned the party was bathed in a warm, flickering candlelight. The bar was set with the ultimate eve of the wedding celebration cocktail, "I Do-tinis," but of course, showcased in framed bar menus, and garnished with personalized drink flags.

The menu was filled with all the traditional backyard bites: southern inspired seasonal salads, summer corn on the cob, barbeque ribs, fennel tomato cabbage slaw, and every possible combination of sides and sauces. And save room for dessert! From southern fruit skillet breads, topped with homemade ice cream, to an infused towering groom's Wii cupcake cake

(adorned with cupcake toppers of his custom Mii and favorite Mario Kart competitors), and the end all be all sweet dream of an ending to the evening: S'mores made 'round the roaring patio firepit, as the starry sky twinkled overhead.

I Do-tini from Inn at Palmetto Bluff
Serves 6

Ingredients:
1 bottle Cachaca 51
1 bottle mango puree
(can also use juice as substitute)
1 bottle limeade

Preparation:
Mix equal parts liquor and juices into a pitcher. Pour into glasses, filled with ice. Garnish with "I Do" straws, our free printable download on www.aperfectevent.com. (See DIY #24)

Farmers' Market Fennel Slaw
from Inn at Palmetto Bluff
Serves 6

Ingredients:
1 red cabbage shredded (can also buy shredded bag, 1 lb.)
1 fennel bulb, trimmed and sliced thin
1 bag shredded carrots
2 scallions, sliced thin
1 container, cherry tomatoes, quartered
1 tsp fresh ginger, minced
2 tbsp. olive oil
2 tbsp. cider vinegar
1/4 c. fresh orange juice
freshly ground pepper

Preparation:
In a bowl, toss cabbage, fennel, carrots, and scallion greens. In a separate bowl, mix together ginger, oil, vinegar and orange

juice; season with black pepper to taste. Pour over slaw, and toss to coat. Refrigerate for 30 minutes to infuse flavors.

Skillet Peach Cobbler

from Inn at Palmetto Bluff

Serves 6

Ingredients:

1/2 t. plus 3 tbsp. butter
1 c. chopped pecan pieces
2 c. diced peaches, peeled
4 large eggs, separated
3 c. half and half
1 1/2 cups yellow cornmeal
1/2 cup freshly grated Parmigiano Reggiano cheese

Preparation:

Preheat the oven to 350°F. Grease a cast iron skilled with 1 teaspoon butter. In a large bowl, whisk the egg yolks and cream together. Add cornmeal and whisk until smooth. Stir peaches and cheese into the cornmeal. Mix until thoroughly combined. In second bowl, whip the egg whites with an electric mixer until very stiff and peaks form, then fold into the peach batter. Pour the batter into the buttered skillet, and bake until it sets, about 45 minutes. Remove from the oven and let stand for 5 minutes. Serve with ice cream or sorbet and fresh berries.

Haute Hostess: When hosting guests for the weekend, in your home, or for an outdoor, seaside event, a welcome box or destination weekend tote bag is the perfect welcome gift. Fill with all those trusted travel necessities, pampering your guests with style and sweet—yet healthy—in-room treats. For our French lavender bug spray, we borrowed a secret recipe from the south of France—using lavender oil as a natural bug repellent. Simply pour it into pretty colored glass bottles, adhere a custom label, and poof—an instant French favor.

Lilly Pulitzer Tea Party

I GREW UP LOVING AND LIVING for Lilly. It was my very own name for Pete's sake—and my grandmother—ever the Jackie O-esque woman of impeccable taste, sophistication, and just an all around fabulous family icon—was always surprising me with handmade Lilly. Every summer, in Petoskey, Michigan, where we floated (literally!) around on the lake with my entire extended family each August, my Gigi would take me into town, where I would pick out my very own Lilly fabric each season. She'd then march down to her sewing room and handmake eyelet edged ditty bags, makeup totes, jewelry pouches...and even some sort of male athletic supporter "pouch" for my baseball stud family member. Ahh, the memories. Love that Lilly.

Imagine my joyful squeal of sheer, thrilling excitement when Jackie asked me to design a Lilly Tea Party Luncheon for her friends and family, before her wedding in Pebble

Beach. Oh, my, did I have the best day ever. Days. Weeks. There were months and months of planning, sourcing Lilly, custom-making tablecloths a la Grandma Gigi, creating petite pennants to be strung across tiny wedding cakes, and more.

Each table was set with a splash of silk, floral Lilly fabric, collections of white depression ware (yet another Gigi favorite) filled with every possible shade of pretty pink petals, silver cake stands filled with tea party treats and sweets, individual silver tea pots, and more. The courtyard of Casa Palmero is a verdant, Moroccan-style chateau setting, complete with a sparkling turquoise swimming pool, oversize cabanas, canvas umbrellas, and of course, a bubbling stone fountain centerpiece. Guests were elated as they arrived for the wedding weekend—welcomed into a floral fantasy of a tea party—and ready to celebrate, girlfriend style.

J + K
ladies tea party
in honor of Jackie
9.2.11

Haute Hostess: The tea party is a real friend to the hard working hostess. Your entire menu can be set on trays, which double as your centerpieces, and dress your tabletop in a delicate, darling display. You aren't stuck in the kitchen, serving—as everything your guests need can be preset at the table. How easy is that?

Stylist Secret: Use architectural features surrounding the party for elevated, thoughtful décor. It is a great tip to bring focal points and drama into the setting, while stretching your budget to highlight installed, available items instead of renting or bringing in new décor resources. Fill fountains and pools with floating flowers—easily designed within minutes—or floating petals, or floating candles...even floating colorful beach balls create a beautiful buzz when adorning bright, blue swimming pools.

Tea Party Menu from Pebble Beach
Serves 6

Ingredients:

Assorted Tea Sandwiches: Smoked Salmon, Egg Salad, Cucumber Dill, Cranberry Chicken Salad

French Pastries, Afternoon Tea Cakes, Petite Fours, Mini Cream Scones served with Strawberry Jam, Lemon Curd, Devonshire Cream

Mini Pennant Cakes served for dessert, in Vanilla "California Dream," Brandy Syrup, Bavarian Cream, Fresh Berries and Whipped Cream

Assorted Teas

Champagne

Coffees

Catering Tip: You can easily source this menu from your grocery, bakery, or make items from scratch. The tea sandwiches and pastry keep easily when prepared 1–2 days in advance.

Cypress Sunset Soirée

THESE DAYS, dinners to celebrate the couple and out-of-town guests, who've traveled in for the weekend celebration the night before the wedding are all the rage. We threw a chic, seaside rehearsal dinner party filled with his and her favorite California cuisine, cocktails, and a themed groom's cake that had everyone talking.

As guests arrived on the west coast, in Pebble Beach, burlap tote bags filled with local, artisanal his and hers favorite sweets and treats were delivered to their room at Spanish Bay. Miette chocolates and bakery bites from San Francisco, Ghirardelli Dark Chocolate Bars, savory popcorn, fresh fruit, local maps, and more was tucked into a tote and tagged with a vintage postcard of Pebble Beach.

Everyone gathered under the glow of the Pacific sunset, candlelight, and an elegant color palette the groom's favorite bright blue. Tabletops on the breezy seaside terrace were

filled with Moroccan lanterns to create warmth, with California pottery filled with local flowers for a beautiful, effortless ambience. Dinner plate Dahlias, Hydrangea, Roses and Ranunculus, all of the bride's favorite florals filled containers and were lined in a long, linear fashion down the table on top of the bright blue burlap runners.

The bride and groom were young, in love, and had very different palates! We designed the party's menu around "Jackie's Favorite" and "Kenny's Favorite" dishes, with special buffet cards to indicate which food was whose fancy.

Jackie's favorites included a nod to her love of Paris—with a French Charcuterie Board: as easy as an oversize wooden cutting board filled with piles of sliced sausage, meats, grilled artichokes, olives and cheese. Toppings of jams, fruit pastes, and tapenades

helped layer and sweeten the beautiful display in French wine bar style. Since the bride had a healthy palate, there was also all things sweet for the groom's palate—including his favorite Callaway Golf Ball baked as a cake, matching "sandtrap" and "putting green" cupcakes, and late-night frosted cake donuts with infused milk shots.

> **Go Green:** In place of designing fresh florals with a short life span for your next party, create glowing luminary and lantern centerpieces. Put candles to aisle to work as the perfect design for table décor, entrances, garden paths, hallways and more. It's pretty, it's easy, and affordable, what more could you ask for?

Charcuterie Board

from Pebble Beach

Gluten Free!

Serves 12

Ingredients:

1 container black olives, pitted
1 container green olives, pitted
1 jar Cornichon, liquid drained, (in grocery aisle, near pickles)
1 lb. thin sliced salami
1 lb. thin sliced Mortadello
1 lb. thin sliced Provolone
1 container quince paste (or similar fruit spread)
1 jar Champagne jelly (in cheese section of grocery, any fruit jam can be used)
1 baguette (I prefer whole grain, can use gluten free if needed)

Preparation:
On a large cutting board, create "mounds" of each taste, with jams and fruit pastes in small bowls, with spreaders for tasting.

Donuts and Milk Shots
from Pebble Beach
Serves 6

Ingredients:
1 c. flour
1/2 c. sugar
1 tbsp baking powder (not baking soda!)
1 egg
1/2 c. milk
1/2 tsp vanilla
4 tbsp cooking oil
icings and sprinkles to your taste

Preparation:
Add all dry ingredients in a bowl, mixing together. Add egg, vanilla, and milk and beat vigorously by hand. Add oil and continue to beat for another minute. Pour batter into a mini donut press, available at all department stores, for fast and easy, perfect little donuts. When brown, remove, and top with melted chocolate, icings, sprinkles, and more. Serve accompanied by milk shots in old fashioned canning jars, available in the grocery aisle. You can flavor the milk with chocolate syrup, strawberry syrup, and more.

Dinner on the Lake

A BEAUTIFUL, turn-of-the-century building on Lake Michigan called Promontory Point set the scene for a magical wedding's eve event. Everyone wants a beautiful, perfect night when celebrating...and this rehearsal dinner was all that and so much more. A gorgeous night on the lake awaited guests, overlooking the fabulous Chicago skyline.

The mother of the groom had requested a beautiful Tuscan evening to celebrate the marriage of her son, Christopher, to his bride, Mychelle, the next day in downtown Chicago. Guests were welcomed into a rustic, outdoor courtyard, with autumnal Tuscan wreaths, adorned with sunflowers and flowing ribbons.

Cocktails outside fêted the bride and groom. Friends and loved ones spoke excitedly about the windy city weekend, and the next day's nuptials, while sipping champagne under the stars and a perfect September sky.

Soon, guests moved inside for a grand Italian dinner. An oversize, vintage chalkboard announced the evening's menu, handwritten in chalk. Each guest found his or her tablecard arranged in repurposed wine-cork holders, which had been gathered for months from the couple's personal pre-wedding celebrations as a thoughtful, recycled collection.

On the tables, organic autumnal Grapevine was designed with fresh fruits, vegetables and flowers tucked about, wrapped around glowing, bronze lanterns. A collection of glass votive candles completed the warm and wonderful effect. A beautiful jar of Italian market fresh pesto at each placesetting, tied with a grosgrain ribbon, served as a favor for guests.

An Italian feast was served family-style, including: baby spinach salad with crispy pancetta; Caesar salad; chicken breast with

sage butter; cheese ravioli with zucchini; and farfalle with cherry tomatoes, asparagus and mushrooms. A magnificent antipasto bar completed the menu, with a variety of breads, meats, cheeses and olives.

Friends and family of the happy couple made many toasts during dinner, and Christopher and Mychelle shared their love of friends, family and the weekend wedding as they toasted with gratitude to everyone who traveled from near and far in celebration.

Then it was time to go back outside, for more drinking and dancing. A family favorite—cappuccino—was designed as a vintage copper bar, serving guests delightful coffees. Dessert was baked in the form of a "giant" New York Giants football helmet cake, in honor of the groom's favorite team. We toasted to tomorrow, when Christopher and Mychelle would be finally be married (see page 210).

Grilled Antipasto Display

from Carlyn Berghoff Catering

Gluten Free!

Serves 6

Ingredients:

2 large red bell peppers, sliced into 2" triangle shapes
2 large orange bell peppers, sliced into large triangle shapes
1 yellow squash
1 zucchini
1 bunch asparagus
2 jars Italian salad dressing
1 jar gourmet black olives
1 jar gourmet green olives
1 jar gourmet marinated mushrooms
2 jars pearl onions

Seasonal Savoir-Faire: Use the outdoors and your local community resources and venues to your advantage. We held this party at a Chicago Park District historic building that was beautiful beyond words. There are hidden gems all over your city, which broadens your options when searching for that perfect venue. Think about what you want your party to be, then do some exploring to find that special, memorable spot.

1 lb. parma ham, sliced in long strips
1 lb. proscuitto, sliced in long strips
1 lb. salami, sliced in long strips

Preparations:
Marinate all vegetables in salad dressing for 1 hour. Heat grill, then grill directly on grill for grill marks on vegetables, 5 minutes per side, or till brown. Remove from grill, and let cool. On large platter, arrange vegetables in groups, creating a round circle shape with pie like wedges of each vegetable. Take long strip of meat, and roll into a spiral. In between vegetables, arrange groupings of meats, also by type. Set cocktail forks in a small glass for serving.

Caesar Salad
from Carlyn Berghoff Catering
Gluten Free!
Serves 6

Ingredients:
3 tbsp. Dijon mustard
2 oz. garlic, chopped
4 egg yolks
1/2 c. red wine vinegar
1 tbsp. Worcestershire sauce
1 c. Parmesan cheese
1 quart olive oil
1 t. black pepper
salt to taste
12 c. Romaine lettuce
1 container radishes, chopped
fresh ground pepper

Preparation:
In a large bowl, mix all ingredients except lettuce and radishes. Tear Romaine lettuce into large pieces and place in large bowl. Pour dressing over lettuce and radishes, toss, garnish with fresh ground black pepper. Serve immediately.

chapter seven

WEDDINGS

I JUST LOVE WEDDINGS. They are, in my opinion, the ultimate party. They are done with an elegance and energy that, often, only comes around once in a lifetime. Today, weddings have become a very personal affair. Most brides and grooms want a celebration that reflects their personality, their style and their story of falling in love. While many couples are continuing traditions of the past, the traditional rulebook about weddings has been all but replaced by celebrations that are fresh, fun, and deeply meaningful to the two people planning them. Love that.

Live-action tasting bars with chefs finishing each small plate by hand—as food centric entertainment—is replacing the traditional seated dinner. Favors are going the way of charitable donations or organic, locavore, artisan sweet treats. And after-parties and after-after-parties are now de riguer, an integral part of the wedding-planning process. The best weddings are all about the season and what's personal to a couple. I'm so happy when a bride brings a sense of personality to her wedding planning, because it's the tiny, unexpected details that make for the most unforgettable nights.

In this chapter you'll find:

From the save-the-date to the final parting moment, it's easy to make a wedding everything you've dreamed of—and so much more. Whether a lavish, black tie city wedding for five hundred or a highly personalized DIY backyard wedding for fifty, the goal is the same: create a wedding to remember, for you, your one true love, and all of the friends and family who have come together to celebrate you. The new wedding is exactly what you want, and boy oh boy do we love to help get you there.

Lovely in the Low Country

I HAVE ALWAYS HAD A LOVE AFFAIR with the South. Steeped in tradition, so gracious, so elegant, so historic. And the food! But I didn't know how to really love the South until I was transported on a wave of true love to the inspiring, idyllic Inn at Palmetto Bluff. I had arrived—I was literally living inside one of my favorite films. I was standing on the soil of the storied deep South, just like Tara, in *Gone with the Wind.*

I love everything old—everything preserved—saved from the wrecking ball. Both my home and A Perfect Event's studio were doomed to destruction until we came along and saved them. And that's one of the amazing, cherished bits of history of Palmetto Bluff.

On a 20,000-acre plantation, 10,000 years of history have been handcrafted to create the most magical resort experience we have ever seen. Centuries old legacies of living well and plantation life are yours for the

taking, linking our present to our storied past. The Lowcountry's land, rivers, seaside white planked cottages, wandering trails, bikes and fishing poles delivered to your door, three story tree houses, world class dining, and oh so much more are at your fingertips.

Our beautiful bride fell in love with Palmetto Bluff, and knew it's romantic, historic magic was the perfect fit for their wedding celebration, bringing family and friends from all over the country together in unison for a long weekend in the South.

This wedding was so deeply touching, so thoughtful, so elegant—I get tears in my eyes just thinking about the beauty, the couple, the scenery, the dolphins swimming outside my cottage door, the ring of the bike bells as guests rode cheerily past in the village—harkening back to the thrill of the good ol' days, and simpler times.

A long Low Country weekend was designed, with meticulous detail, by the bride for her handsome groom, their families, and their closest friends. Our design studio was wrapped, packed, and drove for days to South Carolina. More crew planed, trained, and automobiled to join the road trip. Southern jute, bamboo handled tote bags were filled with southern sweets, treats, custom first aid kids, lavender bug spray, custom crosswords and pencils, and everything guests could possibly want for during their long weekend.

Daily gifts were baked fresh, wrapped in gilded boxes, and delivered. Thousands of white, ivory and champagne flowers, hundreds of sparkling crystal chandelier chains, dozens of towering crystal vases, and more created layer upon layer of dreamy details. After dinner the dance floor opened, a club DJ took stage, the lighting changed to a deep sapphire a la late night club, the veranda revealed a hand rolled cigar bar, front porch chocolate bar, late night milkshakes and sliders, while coordinated custom colored fireworks lit the sky overhead. It was a weekend that we never, ever will forget.

Ocean Blue Cocktail
from Inn at Palmetto Bluff
Serves 6

Ingredients:
1 bottle Absolut peach vodka
1 bottle Blue Curacao
1 bottle Triple Sec
1 jug fresh lemonade
1 jug fresh limeade

Preparation:
Into pitcher, mix 1 part liquors, with 2 parts juices. Can adjust juices to taste. Serve chilled, in glasses.

Stylist Secret: One of the most beautiful ways to bring the tradition of "something old" to your wedding day? Incorporate mom, or grandmother's wedding dress fabric into your wedding details. We love to cover the bridal clutch with lovely lace or silk, and finish the design with an heirloom broach, or fusion of jewels fused together into one feature accent at the center. Another favorite trick—wrap dad or grandfather's handkerchief around your bouquet. One more—embroider or calligraphy silk ribbons with your bridal party's monograms, and add these personalized accents to their bridal party bouquets.

Celebration in the City

A SPRING WEDDING is always my very favorite time of year. And I'm not the only one. More than seven hundred gorgeous guests gathered for the wedding of Sharyl and Michael. Both Chicago natives, the bride and the groom had planned a day of romantic, old-world elegance to celebrate their marriage, with all of their friends and loved ones on hand to witness and to feast on their happiness.

The candlelit ceremony and reception took place inside the legendary, spectacular Hilton and Towers downtown Chicago, situated in Grant Park, in their gorgeous turn-of-the-century ballroom. A large floral arbor was the focal point for the ceremony, and later the backdrop for the band, where it adorned the stage as guests danced (and boy—did they ever dance!) the night away. An arching

frame of flowering branches and curly willow branches were adorned with fresh, climbing vines, ivies, and huge blooms of garden roses and hydrangeas.

After the bride and groom said "I do," everyone moved into the Normandie Lounge, for cocktails and more overlooking the park and city skyline. At the entrance, servers awaited with silver trays of champagne, specialty martinis and sparkling water. Stylist Secret: Greeting guests with drinks as they arrived meant there was no worrying about where to find the bar among the sea of guests, and no waiting once guests found the bar—creating a warm welcome for all.

We used beautiful, old-fashioned English

Garden seasonal flowers throughout the event, creating a magical enchanted garden feel—even while inside a hotel ballroom. A soft, spring palette of warm, antiqued golds and lush green, was combined with touches of white and cream. Silk shantung linens in gold dressed the tables. The couple's elegant monogram, done in ivory and gold, could be found on everything from the cocktail napkins to the programs.

During cocktails, guests chose from a variety of the couple's favorite martinis served from bars made entirely out of ice. From made-to-order "Pineapple Upside Down Cake Martinis," "Lemon Basil Martinis," "Pinky Como Martinis" to, of course, "The Classic Martini," with everyone's favorite: blue-cheese-stuffed olives. Guests also noshed on fabulous fare from chef tasting bars of sushi and sashimi, antipasto, as well as passed hors d'oeuvres.

Soon, guests moved back into the transformed Grand Ballroom for a seated dinner for 700. The room was steeped in romantic candlelight that glowed, flickering on top of golden raw silk tabletops. The same buttercream-colored blooms of hydrangea, spray roses, and orchids, with accents of lush camellia, hypericum berry, and lemon leaves, sat atop tall, gold candle stands as centerpieces. Each guest found a miniature wedding cake at his or her place, wrapped in a square box with ribbon and monogrammed label.

The delicious and simple menu included an appetizer trio, with a Caprese tower, petite fall greens bundled with a cucumber band, and a chilled silver fork wrapped with a single bite of sesame noodle salad. Guests had their choice of sea bass or filet mignon, with potato dauphinoise, as an entree.

After toasts and dancing, the guests enjoyed a trio of desserts: a chocolate pot de crème, a piece of wedding cake and a chocolate box filled with tiramisu. A color coordinated candy bar and cappuccino bar opened in an adjoining Dessert Lounge.

As the dancing continued into the wee hours, servers filled the room with platters of mini-cheeseburgers and french fries to nourish guests for the after-party, which began promptly in the Presidential Suite upstairs at 1:00 a.m. Fortunately, a late morning brunch the next day promised relief, and plenty of coffee, for all.

Go Green: While you're drinking and celebrating, you might as well help save the environment—use Vodka 360, an environmentally friendly super premium vodka, for serving those hundreds of wedding guests. The packaging is all green, with 85 percent recycled glass, 100 percent recycled paper and recyclable cork stoppers that, if returned to the company, McCormick Distillery, will translate to a $1 donation to the environment for each one that's returned (and be sanitized and reused for a future bottle). Now that's a responsible indulgence.

Lemon Basil Martinis
from Chicago Hilton and Towers
Serves 6

Ingredients:
2 bunches fresh basil (thyme is also a favorite)
1 gallon, fresh all-natural lemonade
1 bottle, citrus vodka
1 bottle, natural ginger beer
lemon, sliced into thin rounds
ice

Preparation:
In a martini shaker, muddle (crush with a muddling tool, or back of a spoon) 5 leaves of basil. Add in equal parts lemonade, vodka, ginger ale, and ice. Shake. Pour into chilled martini glasses, and garnish with sliced lemon wheel and a stem of fresh basil.

Mickey's Sugar Cookies

from Take the Cake

My dear friend, Mary Winslow, owner of Chicago's Take the Cake, Inc., started with the idea of baking one wedding cake per month to help pay for her children's college education. That was more than ten years ago and Mary, whose children are now fourteen and seventeen, has established one of the most sought-after sweets businesses in the wedding industry. Here's her recipe for sugar cookies, based on her close friend, Mickey's, original recipe, which she used to make the unforgettable wedding cake cookies we gave to guests as favors at this wedding (see DIY #19).

Makes approximately four-dozen regular cookies or 20 cookie cakes.

Ingredients:
8 3/4 oz. sugar
1/2 lb. (two sticks) unsalted butter, room temperature
1 3/4 ounce large egg
1/4 t. salt
1/2 t. baking soda
15 oz. all-purpose flour
1 t. vanilla

Preparation:
Cream butter and sugar well. Add egg, vanilla and sifted dry ingredients. Chill dough in a bowl or wrapped in plastic wrap in the refrigerator for about twenty minutes. Roll out dough on a lightly floured surface to a thickness of about 1/4-inch and cut into desired shape using a lightly floured cookie cutter. Transfer to a baking sheet lined with parchment paper. Bake at 350°F for 10 minutes, or until a light golden brown (cookies will not get very brown).

DIY #19: The Wedding Cake Cookie

The miniature wedding cake cookies used as favors at this event were adorable—and delicious. They also happen to be easy to make ahead of time. Use the Sugar Cookie recipe on page 200.

Purchase three graduated-size circular cookie cutters. I recommend 3/8", 3/4", and 1" sizes.

Prepare sugar cookie dough. Cut equal numbers of small, medium and large cookie dough rounds, according to the number of your guests. (One of each size round per guest.)

Bake your rounds according to the instructions on page 200. Cool.

Working in an assembly line, lightly frost one large round, one medium round, and one small round. Stack on top of each other (large on the bottom, medium in the middle and small on top).

Repeat for all of your rounds. Allow the cookies to set for a few hours or overnight.

Using your food coloring marker, draw a design on the top cookie round. This can be a small flower, polka dots or even the couple's tiny initials, if you can do it!

A Seaside Celebration

AHH...I GET CARRIED AWAY just thinking about this divine, decadent destination wedding. Pebble Beach, baby. The picturesque peninsula that golfers dream of, while we lucky ladies walk the pounding surf beaches, watching the sunset over the Pacific as the bagpiper strolls and croons across the misty moors.

My Jackie, as I call her, booked Pebble Beach sight unseen. Now that my friends, is love. Her groom loves his golf. And golfers love Pebble Beach. He, like every good golfer, pictured their wedding ceremony, alongside the infamous 18th hole of Pebble Beach, golf's most famous, Pacific waves crashing, Cypress covered course.

So off we went—dozens of boxes loaded, trucks packed, making our way on land and sea across the good ol' US of A headed to the sunshine state. Pebble Beach is heaven on earth.

The ceremony was seaside on the cliffs of

Carmel Bay overlooking the bobbing sailboats dotting the Pacific. Incorporating the bride's Scottish heritage, a bagpiper led the guests along the cart path, from The Lodge to The Beach Club around the point. There, Dom Perignon was poured—until we exhausted the entire resort's inventory—while an oversize Raw Bar sat beside a crackling fire on the terrace, overlooking the harbor as the sunset. Inside the dining room, thousands of local lavender and plum hydrangea, antique roses, sweetpeas, and other soft, summer blooms filled silver urn collections on tables covered in lilac silk, and carved stone mantles. After a four-course, five-star meal, a Parisian Crepe Bar opened in the library, for the ultimate ending to the meal of a lifetime.

For four days, by golly, we celebrated side by side, on the shores of Northern California, surrounded by love, laughter, and happily ever after.

French Crepe Bar
from Pebble Beach
Serves 6

Ingredients:
1 c. all-purpose flour
1/2 c. milk
1/2 c. water
2 eggs
1/4 t. salt
2 tbsp. butter, melted
fresh fruit to vary, including strawberries, raspberries, blueberries, blackberries, pears, apples
fresh herbs to vary, including mint, thyme, rosemary
toppings to vary, including whipped cream, Greek yogurts, nutella, chocolate sauce, caramel

Preparation:
In a mixing bowl, whisk together the flour and eggs. Add in the milk and water, whisking to combine thoroughly. Add salt and butter; mixing until smooth. Heat a lightly oiled griddle or pan over medium heat. Pour batter onto griddle, using approximately 1/4 cup for each crepe. Cook crepe for about roughly 2 minutes, till edges turn light brown. Loosen gently with a spatula, flip, and cook other side. Remove from griddle, fill with fresh fruit and toppings, folding edges on top and filling to cover. Serve hot.

DIY # 20: Party Playlist
My Jackie is a serious superfan—an official, card carrying, VIP member of Celine Dion's uber fan club. As such, she made sure to inject her BFF Celine into every single minute of the prep and the party. How? She made fun, inspired iPod playlists to blast in the bridal suite, getting ready hair and makeup party, in the shuttle around the resort for bridal party photos, during band breaks, and of course during the after party. Concert videos made girlfriend and hotel together time all the more precious, personal, and memorable. Music is transforming—so make a playlist to celebrate every single minute. I remember, clear as a bell,

fourteen years ago, my maid of honor and I belting out "Going to the Chapel" en route to my own wonderful wedding ceremony.

DIY # 21: Floral Monogram

A favorite, gorgeous, memorable focal point, upon entering the party, is a blooming garden monogram. Draw first onto a piece of paper the monogram that you wish to design. Using a rectangular sheet of Styrofoam as a base, cover the top with bricks of floral oasis, that has been submerged in water until "full" (when it sinks below the surface). With

floral tape, wrap the bricks securely to the Styrofoam base, to create one, solid work surface. Using round, fluffy floral blooms to coordinate to your party (I love carnations, roses, and hydrangea), design the two one or letter monogram in the center of the foam. Fill in, around the monogram, with coordinating colored florals, to create a background and fill the space. If using hardy blooms like carnations, this can be made several days in advance, sprayed with water to keep moist, wrapped in clear plastic (a garbage bag works well) and kept cool.

Antique Ambience

IT WAS A GORGEOUS FALL WEDDING for Mychelle and Christopher, the day after their Tuscan-themed rehearsal dinner overlooking Lake Michigan (see page 182).

A very vintage, very chic wedding was on the agenda. The day began with an early-afternoon ceremony at the historic Old Town icon: St. Michael's Church. The special floral details set the tone from front doors of the stunning church, with beautiful wreaths. Inside, flowers in ivory and green were accented with vintage pheasant feathers and striped grosgrain ribbon, in Tiffany blue and brown.

A fabulous celebration awaited at Chicago's turn of the century Murphy Auditorium, a gorgeous building in the French Renaissance style that had been recently restored to its 1920's glory. Immediately upon arrival, guests were served champagne and hors d'oeuvres. A variety of European gourmet

tastes were satisfied, with items like seared foie gras with port wine jelly on sourdough toast points, red grapes rolled in goat cheese and chives, and blue cheese shortbread topped with cream cheese and mango salsa.

This reception was a fun cocktail celebration that spilled out onto the terrace, all the better to enjoy a beautiful September night. Cocktail tables were designed with mossy garden pots and silver julep cups filled with rounded hydrangeas, English garden roses, freesia and more feathers. Vintage silver trophy and loving cup centerpieces dressed the tables, along with handmade paper cake toppers standing atop glass cake stands, with moss, fresh flowers and feathers, all underneath a glass garden cloche. Trios of votives tied with pale blue ribbon surrounded the centerpieces.

As the dining room doors opened, guests moved into the ballroom for dinner and

dancing. The band of course was playing in joyous revelry—and instead of grabbing a chair for dinner, guests moved directly to the floor to start dancing. It was designed as a roving, small plates tasting party than a traditional sit-down dinner, with loads of flavors, chef action bars, and mixing and mingling.

Party tip: Make sure to arrange special seating for guests who have come long distances from out of town and also older guests who want to be seated together and spend time with family.

Breathtaking and dramatic centerpieces were found on each table. Thirty-inch topiaries were potted inside of greenish-brown garden urns, and tied with chocolate-colored silk ribbons. Silver julep cups potted with hints of pheasant feathers and champagne blooms surrounded the topiary.

Guests enjoyed tasting throughout the favorite foodie chef stations—featuring all of the couple's personal gourmet bites. A special southwestern station celebrated the bride and groom's alma mater, Southern Methodist University, with a variety of quesadillas, mini-tacos, and a guacamole bar. Custom designed SMU-themed candle filled lanterns flanked the buffet. Other stations included a Chicago-style steak bar; a seafood raw bar, with oysters, shrimp and maki rolls; and a french fry bar, with traditional and sweet potato fries, and the most delicious toppings you could imagine, from brown sugar to mayonnaise and malt vinegar.

All of the delicious food was announced with custom designed menus, set inside vintage pots and attached to twigs, which appeared as tasty topiaries, just like the centerpieces. The bride's father personally paired his favorite wines with every station, displayed in frames for guests to read tasting notes, choose from and enjoy.

Little List: Make a wedding celebration a reflection of your personal style with vintage details that you collect beforehand, for flower arrangements, buffet tables and centerpieces. Finding an eclectic mix is the beauty of this approach, and creates a singular look for your big day. It's a fun project to begin soon after you get engaged—and don't be surprised if it takes several months to complete.

4 Months: Solidify the décor plan for your wedding, including your color palette, florals, and any other personal theme you may be including. Count out the hard goods you want to collect. It may be just a few centerpieces or it may be pieces for the whole event. Items you want to look for may include: Pots, urns, or vases for floral arrangements. Trays or bowls for food and drink. Votive candle holders for decoration. Cake stands, garden cloches and cake toppers for the centerpieces we did at this wedding. (See DIY #45.)

3 Months: Actively scour flea markets, eBay, garage sales, the grocery, and the collections of family and friends for your vintage hard goods.

2 Months: Conclude your search for your vintage details and order what you didn't manage to find. If you're making the cake-topper centerpieces we did for this wedding, buy your sheet moss and ribbons, according to your wedding's color. Remember, you want a wide ribbon to tie around the bottom of the cake stands or the top of your garden cloche, if there is one, and a narrower ribbon to tie around your votives.

1 Month: Finalize your table count so you know how many pieces you need.

2 Weeks: Package and label all of your vintage pieces (e.g., centerpieces for cocktail tables, trays for servers, vases for buffet tables, etc.). Provide sketches of how the pieces should be used at your reception, and designate someone to be in charge of arranging them on the day of your wedding, whether it's your wedding coordinator, florist or an exceptionally organized friend (certainly not the bride).

Day of: Revel and enjoy the beauty of your custom vintage details, wherever you chose to use them.

It was a high-energy night of wedded bliss, with much celebration and conversation as guests meandered through the fabulous venue, both inside and outside. Dessert, for those who had room (how is that even possible?), included a variety of miniature tiny sweet treats, including petite root beer floats, candied caramel lady apples and warm, sugared donut holes.

But wait—there's more! Gourmet mini-cheeseburgers and, of course, mini-Reubens, were passed on the dance floor late-night. Each guest left with fresh, warm, French macaroons from the couple's favorite French bakery wrapped with ribbon inside of beautiful gift boxes, with a feather and a monogrammed tag tucked in for the perfect farewell.

Caramel Lady Apples

from Carlyn Berghoff Catering

Serves 12

Ingredients:

12 Lady apples or other small-variety apples, washed and dried

12 cinnamon sticks

2 tubs caramel dip for apples (found in the produce aisle at most grocery stores)

A metal skewer or other object to narrowly core your apples

Your choice of toppings:

sprinkles

chocolate shavings

miniature M&Ms

crumbled toffee

ground peanuts or pecans

Preparation:

Using a metal skewer or other object that is similar in width to a cinnamon stick, drill a hole about 3/4 of the way through the core of each apple. Insert one cinnamon stick into each apple. (It's best to do one apple first, to make sure your utensil is the right size and the cinnamon stick stays in place.) On a cookie sheet lined with wax paper, line up your apples with the cinnamon sticks in them. On a second cookie sheet, arrange your topping in a layer across the tray. If you're using several toppings. arrange several trays. Spread the toppings evenly across the bottom of the cookie sheet. You can mix toppings together for some apples, or do one half of the apple in one topping and the other half in another topping. Pour your caramel dip into a microwave-safe bowl and heat until it has a liquid consistency, about 1–2 minutes, depending on your microwave's wattage. Dip your apples into the bowl of caramel one at a time and roll across one or more toppings. Place the apple on the original cookie sheet to set overnight. Repeat for all apples. For an elegant look, knot a ribbon around each cinnamon stick once your apples have set.

French Fry Bar

Serves 6

Ingredients:

French fries:

Choose two packages of your favorite french fry varieties from the freezer section at your grocery store. I like: waffle fries, sweet potato fries, wedges, tater tots, or the traditional french fry.

Toppings:

I suggest serving at least five toppings with your two varieties of fries:

warm melted cheese
brown sugar
ketchup
blue cheese dressing
ranch dressing
remoulade
malt vinegar
garlic salt
chopped chives
truffle aioli
brown mustard
grated parmesan cheese
chopped bacon
12 paper cones, available as snow-cones at a party goods store or make your own with parchment or white card stock (see DIY #16, page 129).
12 water glasses

Preparation:

Arrange your french fry cones in water glasses, so they remain upright. It looks pretty to display them on a tray, or simply on a table. Prepare your toppings beforehand in a variety of containers. I like to use mini-martini-glasses, relish dishes or an eclectic mix of pieces. If you're doing temperature-sensitive ingredients, like melted cheese or salad dressing, prepare just before you're serving your guests. Cook your french fries according to the package instructions. Scoop into your ready-made cones and serve immediately, alongside your toppings. Stylist Secret: Keep these warm in the oven until guests arrive…they get cold much too quickly.

Rustic Barn Romance

C
MACHINE SHED

THE MOST INTIMATE, ROMANTIC wedding celebration was held in historic Barrington, a beautiful town north of Chicago with bucolic green grass rolling hills and white wooden horse-farm fences. I like to say a drive through town is like taking a vacation... from my city neighborhood, that is.

Dylan and his bride, Kelly, were high school sweethearts. Don't you just love that? As such, almost forever and a day they had been planning an unforgettable day to celebrate their marriage. It began with a ceremony in the backyard of the groom's childhood home. Now, I am not kidding, this was like Snow White's cottage—it was just beyond enchanting. Including a swinging half door, country style, that I wanted to immediately unhinge and take home with me.

Guests arrived and picked up ivory program pouches on the way to their seats, which had fresh rose petals tucked inside to toss

overhead the bride and groom as they walked down the aisle.

Thousands of autumnal rose petals and fall foliage carpeted the aisle, while vintage copper buckets were filled with flowers and hung from the chairs where guests were seated. In a sisterly bridal party—the bride's three sisters stood on her side and the groom's sisters stood on his. The couple's darling, demure dog, Buckley, was the ring dog. The bridal party attendants wore fresh floral bracelets, simply made from orange silk ribbons and small orchid blooms. Soon, Kelly walked down the aisle in a vintage lace gown, and underneath a custom-made arbor of birch tree trunks, hanging amaranthus, and more flowing orange ribbons, Kelly and Dylan read their personal vows to each other.

After the ceremony, the bride and groom happily hopped into a vintage MG, tied with tin cans and all, zooming over the hills and through the fields, to the romantic reception. They had found a magical, empty country barn located on an idyllic hillside—the perfect site for a nightlong celebration.

As guests arrived, orange paper lanterns hung from oversized trees in the cocktail field. Underneath, a French fondue bar in vintage copper pots was served, with bubbling cheeses, sausages, breads and vegetables, with cocktails overlooking the countryside. Guests found their placecards, little chalkboard slates tucked into twine wrapped around a big, beautiful tree and made their way into the barn for the reception.

A winding path, covered with mismatched oriental rugs and lit with lanterns, pumpkins and potted mums, led the way to the barn. On the outside of the barn doors, a large, mossy K and D hung on the side in celebration of the couple. Inside the barn, huge chandeliers and candles had been installed everywhere. Pillar and votive candles ran along the rafters for a glow throughout the room. A rustic "hayloft lounge," was designed, with oriental rugs, distressed leather sofas and farmhouse style coffee tables.

The dining tables were dressed with custom silk linens in pecan brown, barn red, persimmon and copper. A trio of copper pots, vintage vases and watering cans adorned each table. Seasonal blooms of dinner plate dahlias, zinnias, roses, and berries filled the containers in the

warm, autumnal hues. A collection of eclectic, vintage votive candles in rich, jewel tone colored glass surrounded the florals on each table.

A signature barn icon with the bride and groom's names was at the top of the evening's menu, tucked into rust-colored napkins on amber glass charger plates. Guests feasted on potato leek soup in petite pumpkins and a baby greens salad, with goat cheese soufflé; pumpkin seed–crusted chicken, with sage stuffing and baked apples; and a dessert "amuse" of milk and doughnut, caramel Lady apple and blueberry pie. The wedding cake was a cupcake cake, with monogrammed chocolate hearts.

Guests danced the night away to Bill Pollack's Chicago Motown band. The groom himself was a musician and in loving tribute to his new wife, wrote the couple's first dance, singing it to her as they danced along to the band. Later in the night, guests moved outside to the fire pit for S'mores and a barnside haybale "lounge."

Fondue Trio

from Blue Plate Catering

Serves 12

Ingredients:

Vermont's Best Cheddar Fondue:

2 garlic cloves, lightly crushed
2 tbsp. unsalted butter
3 tbsp. dry white wine
1 tbsp. cornstarch
12 oz. cheddar cheese, coarsely grated
Accompaniment: French bread, sliced brats, broccoli florets, fingerling potatoes

Gorgonzola Dolce Fondue:

2 garlic cloves, lightly crushed
2 tbsp. unsalted butter
3 tbsp. dry white wine
1 tbsp. cornstarch
12 ounces gorgonzola dolce cheese, crumbled
Accompaniment: dried figs, walnut raisin bread, seedless grapes

Gruyere Fondue:

2 garlic cloves, lightly crushed
2 tbsp. unsalted butter
3 tbsp. dry white wine
1 tbsp. cornstarch
12 oz. gruyere cheese, shredded
Accompaniment: rye bread chunks, cauliflower florets, cherry tomatoes

Preparation:

For each fondue recipe, cook garlic in butter in a 4-quart heavy saucepan over moderately low heat, stirring occasionally, until most of liquid is evaporated, about 5 minutes. Stir together wine and cornstarch in a small bowl, then stir into butter and simmer gently, stirring, 1 minute. Discard garlic. Add specified cheese by handfuls, stirring until completely melted. Serve each fondue in a fondue pot set over a flame, with accompaniments.

Potato and Leek Soup in Petite Pumpkins

from Blue Plate Catering

Serves 12

Ingredients:

2 large leeks, chopped
20 black peppercorns
4 sprigs fresh thyme
2 tbsp. butter
2 strips bacon, chopped
1/2 c. dry white wine
5 c. chicken stock
1 to 1 1/4 lb. russet potatoes, diced
1 1/2 t. salt
3/4 t. white pepper
1/2 to 3/4 c. crème fraîche or heavy cream
12 petite pumpkins
6 oz. white truffle oil

Preparation:

With a spoon, hollow out petite pumpkins, carefully making sure that all the flesh and seeds are removed. Set aside. In a large soup pot over medium heat, melt the butter and add the bacon. Cook for 5 to 6 minutes, stirring occasionally, until the bacon is very soft and has rendered most of its fat. Add the chopped leeks and cook until wilted, about 5 minutes. Add chicken stock, potatoes, salt and white pepper, and bring to a boil. Reduce the heat to a simmer and cook for 30 minutes, or until the potatoes are falling apart and the soup is very flavorful. Remove the thyme and, working in batches, puree the soup in a food processor or blender. (Alternately, if you own an immersion blender, puree the soup directly in the pot.) Stir in the crème fraîche and adjust the seasoning, if necessary. Fill pumpkins with hot soup and drizzle with truffle oil.

Seasonal Savoir-Faire: For a warm-weather wedding, use floral ribbon bracelets for readers, greeters and other special bridal party attendants. It's a wonderful, fresh alternative to traditional corsages. Just take a length of ribbon and a few fresh blooms (we used orange mokara orchids), adhere with a hot glue gun, cool, and tie around the wrist.

DIY #22: Copper Aisle Buckets

We created festive copper bucket pieces with orange silk ribbons as handles, which we hung from the chairs during the ceremony and repurposed as centerpieces at the reception. These multi-purpose pieces are a great way to add seasonal color to a wedding and extend your floral budget.

Purchase or gather the needed number of small (4–6" in diameter) copper buckets. We hung one bucket on the aisle chair of every other row, then reused them as centerpieces at the reception (along with other floral pieces). You can also use enamel, silver or galvanized metal containers, if they are easier to find or work better with your wedding palette.

Purchase 24 inches of ribbon for each container, in a color of your choice. We used orange silk ribbons for this wedding. Remember, this needs to be sturdy, good-quality ribbon, since the potted buckets will be hanging from them.

Purchase floral oasis and blooms, available at your local crafts store or florist, according your wedding design. We used autumnal colors of dahlias, zinnias, and roses, with berries for accent.

The day before the wedding, cut your floral oasis so one piece fits inside the bottom of each container.

chapter eight

ANNIVERSARIES

OF ALL THE EVENTS that are important to cherish in our lives, I think an anniversary is perhaps the most special. Whether a wedding or a corporate milestone, an anniversary is a marker of where we've been and also where we're going. It's not a once-in-a-lifetime celebration, but rather a lifelong celebration of our finest accomplishments.

I like the idea of celebrating anniversaries regularly. I think it gives a sense of belonging to everyone who's connected to the anniversary, whether friends, children, or other special people. Making important anniversaries a regular part of our lives doesn't have to be complicated. In fact, it's good to have some fun, plan a casual party and enjoy the moments in our lives where we can take a step back and say...we did it. Bravo!

We all deserve to celebrate and cherish the defining moments in our lives as often as we can.

In this chapter you'll find:

- *A 110th Anniversary*
- *A Toast to Friendship*
- *A Perfect 10*

A 110th Anniversary

IT'S ALWAYS A MOMENTOUS celebration when a couple reaches their 60th wedding anniversary. And, when a couple reaches their 40th. Likewise, when a young couple reaches their 10th. And what better way to celebrate than with an updated version of not simply the original day, but all three original wedding days, combined into one triple 110th celebration?

A beautiful, French bistro-infused evening of elegance was held at Chicago's Madame Tartine—to cherish the union of my dear grandparents, my parents, and my own wedding anniversaries. Ten years ago, on the eve of the eve of my own wedding, Mike and I threw a surprise anniversary party for my parents and grandparents. It was such a fun, shock and surprise to the guests of honor, who thought we were simply meeting for a pre-nuptial weekend dinner. When they walked in—there was all of our extended family, and out of town

friends, in early to surprise them in celebration. It was, by far, one of the highlights of my wedding weekend.

This anniversary occasion was all about recreating and updating each couple's wedding day, including many of the photographs and décor details of the original days, personalized and tucked into every nook and cranny. Not to mention, these two couples are the reason that I am totally, completely, obsessed with pretty Paris. The six of us (plus my two little ones) had just returned from summer in Paris, including an anniversary dejuner (lunch) to remember always atop Tour Eiffel, a la Jules Verne.

As guests arrived, we flowed into the private dining room for an elegant cocktail soiree. A throw back, 60s Pucci black and white tabletop commemorated the black and white wedding memories from bygone

decades, and set the tone for playful centerpieces and favors.

On this night, dinner was designed as a fun heavy bites cocktail reception for all three of the couple's friends and family. Flutes of French Champagne, French 75s, and passed Parisian hors d'oeuvres were served to the merry guests. For dessert, a black and white, photowrapped candy bar was designed in another spin on the throwback decades.

The black lacquered room, dark paneled and mirrored walls, and glossy bistro tables were set with classic chic details like candlesticks topped with spheres of hydrangea, and filled with candles, creating a warm, cozy ambience.

Guests spent the evening hamming it up in the vintage black and white photo booth, creating a photo strip scrapbook with reflective messages of love and decade long memories handwritten by each guest. All 110 years brought back to life, for just one night.

Haute Hostess: To keep a party flowing perfectly and your guests entertained with fresh colors and details, design the space to move and flow from one moment to the next. Use different color palettes to distinguish different phases of your party, even if it's just from one room of the house to the next. Just when your guests think they've seen everything, another set of doors open and they move into the next phase of the party, with new colors, florals, and themes!

DIY #23: Accordion Books

Pictures are always beautiful and look all the more special when shared together as a story. They can be used to accent cocktail and dinner tables, add personality to center-pieces, and more. Create several unique accordion "photo stories" for added interest.

Decide how many photographs you want to feature, and make sure photo quality is good for high resolution prints.

Purchase accordion books from a stationery or office supply store. Count the pages, and plan accordingly for ordering prints to fill both sides of each series of pages.

If desired, use a cutting board with a patterned blade like a zigzag, scallop, etc. for an elegant, whimsical finishing detail.

Using double sided tape (works better than glue stick for a professional look) adhere photos to each page.

Place around the party for heartfelt tabletop décor, doubling as wonderful keepsakes for the couples to take home at the end of the evening.

A Toast to Friendship

WHAT COULD BE MORE FUN than a group of long, steadfast friends celebrating years of friendship, in the middle of a gorgeous Nantucket summer? We planned in impromptu party for our closest friends and neighbors to celebrate our love for each other, entertaining, and the island. The theme? A lobster boil, of course, held in the backyard of my family's home. I've been in love with the island for a lifetime, surely inherited from my mother, who fell in love with it while pouring over *Moby Dick* in high school. It's where we celebrate every possible family occasion (and honestly, quite often sometimes no occasion whatsoever), every single summer.

This anniversary party was a fun, casual, backyard summertime gathering, which frankly is always my favorite. We invited our neighbors and friends to join us for dinner, and everyone brought their favorite dish to

taste—a modern version of the classic pot luck—and in most cases, a specialty that we have enjoyed together every single summer for years and years.

The result was a gorgeous, chic, yet mismatched table set under a canopy of trees in our backyard. Chairs and settees from inside neighboring homes were tucked around a single, long dining table. Strands of capiz shells were hung from the trees, chiming as they blew in the beachy breeze. Paper lanterns from crisscrossed clotheslines, dangling in darling fashion over the table. Tall, glowing candle lanterns were set on the porch and patio, adding warmth and ambience.

Tabletop, we created the same elegant mix and match mish-mash of pieces. We used a crewel bedspread as our tablecloth. We filled vintage glass vases that we found in town—"treasures" discovered with great glee at an

island tag sale—with bright magenta phlox, a stunning seasonal summer flower.

Cotton napkins were gathered with pearly seashell napkin rings, from my mother's collection. And gorgeous citrus centerpieces provided the easiest beauty. We filled crystal bowls with fresh clementines and lemons from the local farmer's market, and surrounded them with candles in crystal candleholders.

As our guests arrived they mingled in the garden, enjoying a delicious Lillet lemonade cocktail, a specialty of our dear neighbor and Julia Child protege, Ann. The French aperitif was served in small colored glasses brought from her personal collection, and garnished with fresh lime slices. This is now my favorite cocktail to serve every summer.

Heavy hors d'oeuvres were served inside the house on the kitchen table—turned buffet. From my mom's famous, delicious sweet potato hummus, neighbor Jim's smoked salmon on toast points with crème fraîche and capers, and Dad's fabulous charcuterie platter, with cheeses, meats, breads, crackers, and olives, on a large, festive fish-shaped cutting board—an informal feast ensued. Ann contributed another one of her not-to-be-missed specialties—heavenly herbed, spiced nuts, served with bowls of dried apricots and cranberries.

For dinner, we enjoyed our friend E.J. Harvey's Nantucket Clam Chowder, shrimp and sausage paella, and a proper lobster boil, cooked with kielbasa and onions, and served with corn on the cob and corn bread.

The piece de resistance? Ann, while she was sleeping, whipped up the most divine chocolate mousse cake, topped with fluffy white frosting and special chocolate leaves, handmade from the backyard ivies with my seven-year-old daughter, Lilly. There were also island specialty chocolate truffles in the shape of whales, from the town chocolatier. It was an unforgettable night to celebrate our neighbors, family, and a lifetime of wonderful memories, with the help of some cherished friends.

Mom's Sweet Potato Hummus

Gluten Free!   Serves 6

This is one of my favorite recipes—and so pretty to serve on a tasting buffet. It's also one of those dishes that is unsuspectingly nutritious...and delicious. The recipe itself comes from Ann Howard, my favorite caterer in Hartford, Connecticut. Ann's little shop near my parent's home was a big inspiration for me when I was in high school and college. Every holiday visit had me dreaming of party-planning the very second after I graduated.

Ingredients:
1 lb. sweet potatoes
1 t. cumin seeds
1 large lemon, juiced
1 t. salt
1/4 t. cayenne pepper
1/8 t. freshly ground black pepper
1 tbsp. tahini
1 tbsp. olive oil
3 t. brown sugar
zest of one orange
1 t. crumbled feta cheese
1 t. toasted pistachios
pita chips or gluten free corn chips

Preparation:
Bake your sweet potatoes until fully cooked, usually around one hour, depending on the size. A fork will easily pierce the middle of the potato when done. Cool, then remove skins. Over low heat, toast the cumin seeds for a few minutes. Crush the seeds using a mortar and pestle, or by placing in a Ziploc bag and pounding with a heavy object. Combine peeled sweet potatoes and crushed cumin in a food processor. Add lemon juice, salt, cayenne pepper, black pepper, olive oil, brown sugar, orange zest, and tahini. Blend until smooth and creamy. Transfer hummus to a bowl and sprinkle hummus with crumbled feta and toasted pistachios. Serve with pita chips, toast points, sliced baguette or chips.

Ann's Little Lillets

Serves 6

Ingredients:
12 oz. Lillet Blanc
12 oz. Lemonade
12 oz. Club soda
1/2 lime, cut into six thin slices

Preparation:
In a pitcher, combine Lillet, and Lemonade. Chill for one hour (or longer). Pour into aperitif glasses, wine glasses, or other small glasses, such as juice glasses, with a lime slice already inside the glass, and top with a splash of club soda.

DIY #24 Ann's Chocolate Leaves

The beautiful chocolate leaves that topped this cake are so unbelievable easy to make. Ann's simple recipe is a stunner for any dessert, or even on their own, which will wow your guests. Ann taught my daughter how to make these—and now the pressure's really on—it's all Lilly talks about years later.

Gather 16 waxy leaves, with stems, from the backyard, the park or the florist. English ivy leaves, grape ivy leaves or myrtle leaves are all wonderful choices.

Clean your leaves gently by dry brushing them or rinsing and drying. Clip so that at least an inch of stem remains.

Purchase chocolate ingredients: 6 oz. of semisweet chocolate chips and 2 teaspoons of Crisco.

Melt your chocolate and Crisco together. Using a teaspoon, generously coat the back of a leaf.

Place on a cookie sheet lined with wax paper.

Repeat for all leaves.

Transfer the cookie sheet to the refrigerator or freezer and chill until the leaves are firm. Remove from the refrigerator or freezer and separate chocolate from the leaves, starting with the stem of the leaf.

Place leaves on top of cakes, pastries, or serve alone or as favors. These leaves freeze very well in Tupperware containers lined with wax paper and may be prepared several weeks ahead of time.

DIY #25: The Flavorful Favor

My favorite thing is the miniature whale truf-

fles at this party, while my mom's is the spicy, herbed nuts. It's easy to create a memorable anniversary favor, made of a custom food item, with a tag that celebrates the original day.

Choose a recipe that is a favorite of the couple's. This can include a current favorite, or something that was served at the couple's wedding, whether a petite version of their cake, a special candy, or a smaller version of a savory snack.

Decide how you will wrap your favor. Some ideas include: small tins, acrylic boxes, miniature bowls or a glassine bag, widely

available online and at crafts stores. Purchase one container or bag per guest and double check that your containers are the right size for your food item!

Plan on wrapping each favor with ribbon and a custom tag, made of cardstock. One easy way to customize an anniversary party favor is to choose ribbons and/or containers in the original wedding colors.

Seasonal Savoir-Faire: Make the decision to celebrate friendship every year, as a touchstone for you and yours, neighbors, family and friends. Create a tradition and use the season as inspiration. You can even serve the same seasonal menu each year, as a way to commemorate the special day. I think these types of annual gatherings are the most valuable for marking the moment of our lives and give everyone something to look forward to each year.

Purchase coordinating ribbons and cardstock to make your tags. Plan on getting nine tags per piece of cardstock, with a few extra pieces for practice. The amount of ribbon you need will vary according to the size of your container, but 12 inches per favor is a good rule of thumb.

Order or confirm the recipe you will use for your edible favor items.

Create your custom tags. Choose a special detail from the couple's wedding day, such as a picture, their monogram or other wedding detail.

Lay out the tags in a Word document, nine tags to a page. You will want to space the picture, text or artwork evenly in three rows of three.

Print your design onto cardstock and, using a paper cutter, trim to size. Square-shaped tags are the easiest. Circular tags can be done, but should be cut professionally at a Kinko's or similar type of store.

Make a hole at the top of each tag using a hole puncher.

Tie a piece of ribbon around the favor and thread through the tag. Finish in a bow or knot.

Place at each guest's seat or on a favor table.

Visit www.aperfectevent.com/inspirations for event invitation, menu, and placecard templates.

Little List: A memorable party doesn't have to be months in the making. In fact, you can plan just days in advance. Most people love parties, but never get around to throwing them. Sometimes, it's fun to take the pressure off, give up the idea of perfection and just focus on having fun! Here's how to make a last-minute party happen.

1 Week: Decide your guest list, which should include mainly local people, (unless you think someone will feel left out and want to fly or drive in for the event). Send a quick email to the group to tell them that you are having a party. Ask each guest to bring a favorite dish or cocktail and decide what you will make on your own, whether several things or just one thing. Everyone brings his or her items all ready to serve—fast and easy for the hostess. This includes a serving platter and appropriate serving pieces, if needed (glasses, pitcher, plates, etc.).

3 Days: Figure out how you will seat your guests and decorate your table(s). Are there items in other parts of the house that can work as centerpieces? Floral arrangements, statues, candles and just about anything you can put on a table will work. Or go local like we did, and buy inexpensive, seasonal items from a local store or farmer's market. Scour neighbors' or friends' houses and gather chairs or any other items you may need.

Day Before: Set your tables. Prep any food you may be making for the party.

Day of: Finish your dish(es), light the candles and enjoy your fabulous, no-stress party.

A Perfect 10

I RARELY GET TO SPEND TIME planning my own parties, and my entire staff feels the same. But 10 years is a big deal for any small entrepreneur and company. So, amongst all of other client parties during the busy month of August, we decided to throw ourselves a little party of our own, to celebrate ten years of wonderful relationships and thousands of parties around the city of Chicago.

We held the event inside our studio and to accommodate the size of our guest list, also tented the alley behind the building, which gave the evening some movement and variety. This night was all about our employees, our clients and all of the hot décor, detail, and menu trends.

Inside, the color palette was an electric coral. Beautiful glass cylinders were wrapped with a gauzy, coral fabric, for a colorful glow. The centerpieces were short paves of roses, in

corseted vases wrapped in silk, with thin ribbons tightly wound around them. An elegant centerpiece at the entrance, of Granny Smith apples and Cymbidium orchids in a terra cotta pot, said "thank-you" to all of our clients from over the years.

Outside in the tented dessert lounge, we did a lively palette of white and empire green, with flickering candlelight providing the only illumination. Simple arrangements of greens, like monstera leaves, papyrus, and fiddlehead ferns were placed in clear glass vases, with water and river rocks. Candlelight covered the tables and also the ceilings, flickering in white paper lanterns.

The evening's specialty cocktail was sparkling shiraz, the hottest new thing in wine, and "Ten-tinis," of course—a delicious martini to celebrate the anniversary, served with candy cane straws.

Guests were moving inside and outside throughout the space on this picture perfect late-summer night. A variety of wonderful hors d'oeuvres from two of Chicago's best caterers, Food for Thought and Blue Plate Catering, were passed. The nibbles included ceviche spoons, coconut chicken skewers, beef empanadas and ginger scallops. We also had a live-action sushi bar, with chefs from Chicago's Kaze Sushi preparing fresh maki and sashimi for guests.

And what A Perfect Event party would be complete without a decadent candy bar? I had just returned from the south of France, with my suitcase packed full of Marseilles' finest candies, so we did a very French "Bon Bon Bar," with vibrant, vivid Haribo candies in clear glass containers, as well as infused truffles and floral cupcakes with bright, colorful frosting, from Take the Cake. We catered to the wee guests as well, with passed miniature cotton-candy pops, enjoyed by the children and the adults alike.

At the end of the night, we said farewell and toasted to another ten years. As each guest left, a Chicago style hot dog cart waited at the curb, with steaming, juicy hot dogs, complete with all of the Chicago-style fixings, and custom bottled waters on ice, paired with hot coffee to-go. It was the perfect farewell for a company and a party that was all about my favorite town.

Go Green: Give the environment, and your electric bill, a break by opting for candlelight-only at your next party. We used candlelight in the tent, on the tables and in white paper lanterns that hung from the ceiling, for warm, guilt-free ambience. Candles are the perfect way to reduce your carbon footprint and they happen to look great, too.

DIY #26: Fabric-Wrapped Hurricanes
Create instant warmth with fabric-wrapped hurricanes—one of our favorite stylist secrets.

Using three sizes (odd numbers look best in groups) of glass cylinder vases (Debi Lilly Design Illusion Vases at Safeway are my go to choice) , choose 3 yards of sheer organdy fabric in your color palette.

Select a coordinated color ribbon, to wrap around the top and bottom of the cylinder, and down the seam. I love our Debi Lilly Design Satin Ribbon, at Safeway, 1" wide.

How much ribbon do you need? Wrap a tape measure around each cylinder to determine the circumference. Multiply each circumference times two. Measure the length of each cylinder top to bottom, add this to your circumference total. Add about 2 inches for over- lap and any mistakes.

Wrap fabric around each vase, trim to size. The fabric should be flush with the top and bottom edges of the vase, with about one inch of overlap around the body of the vase.

Place a few pieces of double-sided tape along the top and bottom of the vase and in a line down the length of the vase, where the two pieces of fabric will form a seam. Press fabric in place ontop the tape.

Cut your ribbons to size so you have three ribbons for each hurricane or vase: Two for the circumference measurement and one for the length of the vase. You want to have an extra 2–3 inches of length for each ribbon, beyond your original hurricane measurements.

Place double-sided tape along the back of each piece of ribbon. Press one ribbon in place around the top edge of the cylinder, one around the bottom edge of each cylinder, and one along the seam of fabric running down the vase.

Fill the fabric-wrapped hurricanes with candles, we love our Debi Lilly Design pillar candle collection, or with water and floating candles, and light.

chapter nine

PERFECT PARTY BASICS

I LOVE IT when neighbors and friends stop by, and it's the perfect excuse to keep wine chilled and hors d'oeuvres in the pantry or freezer. So, here's what every host or hostess should have on hand for impromptu entertaining. Casual, last-minute gatherings are often the most memorable, and having a few essential supplies can allow you to go with the party planning flow!

The basics of a well-rounded pantry allow you to prepare simple versions of a variety of quick appetizers, meals, and desserts.

Pantry

- Olive oil
- Balsamic vinegar
- Sea salt
- Freshly ground black pepper (coarse ground or peppercorns in a grinder)
- Canned black beans and cannellini beans (the most versatile protein there is!)
- Canned San Marzano tomatoes (the best)
- A variety of crackers, corn chips, and gourmet breadsticks
- Gourmet salsas and queso dips
- Cake or brownie mix
- Chocolate chips
- Raw almonds and cashews

Of course, you can't plan in advance to have enough perishable food items in the refrigerator for guests, but I always like to have:

- Oranges, apples, lemons, and limes
- Cilantro and basil
- Garlic
- A few different types of cheeses
- Hummus
- Pesto
- Chutney
- Mustard, a few varieties

Stocking the freezer with a few essentials increases your party bandwidth significantly:

- Frozen chicken breasts
- Ground turkey (not ground turkey breast)
- Sorbet
- Delicious miniature appetizers from the grocery store freezer aisle

Bar

A stocked bar is a happy bar and allows you to whip up a variety of libations, which always get a party rolling or can be served to unexpected guests:

- Vodka, gin, scotch, and whiskey
- A couple of bottles each of white wine and red wine. Make sure these are stored in a relatively cool area, or put them in the basement.
- A bottle of champagne (you never know when a moment is going to call for celebration!) Keep this on its side in the refrigerator."
- A six-pack each of tonic and club soda. This way you can open individual cans and not waste semi-liters.
- Lime juice (the plastic green "limes" available at the grocery store)
- A martini shaker
- A shot glass, for quick measuring
- Glass pitchers

Don't worry about glasses. I think it's important to have fun and get creative with how drinks are served instead of worrying about everything matching. Drinks can be served in juice glasses or a mishmash of whatever you have if you're fretting about not having margarita glasses, martini glasses, etc.

Centerpieces/Favors

The idea of making a centerpiece or a favor scares off some people, but it's easier than you think. Here are the supply basics for pulling something together, whether you have time to shop or not. I like to keep these items in a closet for easy access, with no running around required.

- A good-quality floral clippers that you only use for flowers
- Floral oasis
- Floral water tubes (small size)
- Several vases in different sizes and even different colors or designs. Just keep them in one place for easy access. You can also use pitchers, decanters, or glasses—everything works.
- Good-quality scissors for paper
- A hole-punch, preferably one small and one large
- A few types of ribbon in different patterns and widths, including at least one roll of double-face satin ribbon
- A few packages of cardstock and paper, in different colors
- Glue and a hot glue gun
- Double-sided tape
- Colorful pens and markers
- Votive candle holders
- A variety of candles: pillar, votive, floating, and taper (I love 18"–24")

Here are some simple guidelines when preparing floral arrangements to extend their beauty:

- Always use clean, sharp floral clippers when cutting flowers. If you don't have one, use a sharp knife. Never use ordinary scissors to cut floral stems, since they destroy the stem's ability to properly absorb water.

- Always cut stems at an angle, which encourages proper water uptake.

- Remove all foliage that will be submerged in water, such as leaves on the lower part of the stems. The arrangement will stay fresh longer by inhibiting the growth of bacteria in the water. (Not to mention keep the water clear and smelling fresh!)

- Fill containers with lukewarm water for most types of flowers. Use cold water for bulb flowers such as tulips, paperwhites, and hyacinth.

- Definitely use the packet of flower preservative that accompanies many arrangements, as they really do extend the life of the blooms by inhibiting the growth of bacteria.

Perfect Party Etiquette

These basics of good entertaining ensure you will be a hostess with the mostest. Create the perfect event. . . It's as easy as 1, 2, 3!

1 **Invitation Impression.** Send invitations at least 4 weeks before your party. The invitation is your first impression and it sets the tone for the party to come. Whether Holidays in Paris or a Backyard BBQ, there is an invitation for every season and every party reason. You don't have to go custom and professional (though it's always fabulous!). Pre-printed and homemade invitations with your own special touch can be just as wonderful. Then, properly address your invitations. Remember these simple rules and you'll be like Emily Post in no time:

- Keep guest names on a single line. For informal parties, first and last names only are fine: John and Jane Smith. Or, The Smith Family.

- For formal or traditional events, address with social titles: Mr. and Mrs. John Smith; or, Mr. John Smith and Mrs. Jane Smith.

- Female guests who are divorced or have retained their maiden name are addressed as: Ms. Jane Smith. When married: Mr. John Smith and Ms. Jane Smith.

- Female guests who are widowed are addressed as: Mrs. John Smith (traditional) or Mrs. Jane Smith (acceptable).

- Female guests under age 18 are addressed as: Miss Jane Smith.

2 Menu Maven. Set your menu to reflect the theme of your event for a festive flair, or to celebrate a special guest of honor's favorite dishes. It doesn't have to be fancy—just a thread that weaves itself through food, drink, and décor for a party to remember. If you're doing the cooking, comfort foods and old favorites often make for the best parties at home. It's also my favorite time to try great new recipes I've never had a chance to prepare before.

I also highly recommend using local gourmet markets for premade items to relieve yourself of some of the cooking burden. If you're not doing the cooking yourself, I recommend finding a reputable caterer and having some fun with your menu! So long as you know someone who's had success with the caterer, chances are good that you can rely on a delicious menu that you wouldn't necessarily know how to prepare yourself. Catered events are great for satisfying a variety of palates and even introducing guests to some new foods.

3 Eat, Drink, and Be Merry. Create a welcoming event for your guests from arrival to departure. Greet guests with a specialty signature cocktail—for example, one of the many "tinis" we served to set the tone at the parties featured in this book. Everyone loves a cocktail and it's an elegant and delicious way to start a party. And as I've mentioned, offering a specialty cocktail, along with some wine and sparkling water, is more fun and festive than offering a full bar. Also, don't forget the "mocktail," the modified version of the drink for guests who are underage, pregnant, designated drivers for the night, or simply don't drink. Just omit the alcohol from a drink recipe or substitute sparkling grape juice for champagne . . . you get the idea.

4 Table Setting Savvy. Many hosts and hostesses fret over how to set a table. What with all the glasses, utensils, and plates, it can be

dizzying. I've got some simple etiquette dos and don'ts that can come to the rescue, whether you're hosting a formal dinner party for 8 or lunch for 30. Do set your table like a pro: forks go to the left of the plate. Here is the easy-to-remember tip I give my in etiquette workshops: f-o-r-k and l-e-f-t both have four letters." Similarly—to help never forget again—knives and spoons go to the right of the plate, with five letters in each knife, spoon and plate. Place flatware in the order it is used, from the outside in. (For instance, salad fork on the outside, dinner fork closest to the plate.)

Don't expect guests to eat a formal, served meal with one plate. Bread plates are a polished touch and are placed above the fork. Do provide the proper kinds of glasses for your guests. Water goblets, white wine glasses, red wine glasses, and sparkling wine glasses are available everywhere, and their unique designs add to the enjoyment of what's inside.

Place water glasses above the innermost knife, with wine glasses to the right. Do provide placecards to indicate seating, which helps to avoid confusion and mix-up seating—encouraging new friends and sparking conversation. Don't serve your guests until everyone's food is ready. Serve from the left and clear (also in concert) from the right. Or, do a buffet, which is fun for guests and easier for you! Do pass the breadbasket or other shared dishes, always to the *right*. Remember b-r-e-a-d has five letters, same as r-i-g-h-t.

5 How to Be the Perfect Guest. If you're more of a *party gal* or *guy* than a *party planner*, here are a few tips to be the perfect guest at any occasion:

- Whether it's to a wedding, a dinner party, a shower, or a gala event, an invitation comes with some important obligations. Reply promptly, within a day or two of receiving an invitation. If the invitation is "Regrets Only," reply only if you cannot attend. Otherwise, your host is expecting you!

- Unless indicated on the invitation or by the host, don't even ask if you can bring a guest! An invitation is extended to the people the hosts want to invite—and no one else. This includes dates, children, houseguests, and foreign exchange students!

- Being a no-show to a party, no matter how informal, is unacceptable if you have not let the host know beforehand. Always call as soon as you know you will not be able to attend a party.

Make sure to thank your hosts before you leave a party, and then again by phone or note the next day.

chapter ten

PERFECT PARTY SOURCES AND SOLUTIONS

HERE IS A LIST of all of the fabulous caterers, venues, photographers, and dramatic details that were part of each of the exquisite events featured in this book. For more information, please visit their websites, work together for your next party and—above all—enjoy them.

Cocktails with Art & Giada, Page 16

- Venue and Caterer: Chef Art Smith, at his home: www.chefartsmith.net
- Photography: Artisan Events www.artisanevents.com

Winter Wonderland, Page 24

- Venue: River East Art Center www.rivereastartcenter.com
- Caterer: J&L Catering www.jandlcatering.com
- Photography: Artist Group www.artistgroup.net
- Entertainment: The Jingle Belles www.frostsounds.com/JingleBelles
- Entertainment: AcRock www.acrock.com
- Entertainment: The Connection www.billpollackmusic.com
- Entertainment: The Second City www.secondcity.com
- Linens: BBJ Linen www.bbjlinen.com

Spa Soirée, Page 32

- Venue: Prairie Production www.prairieproduction.net
- Caterer: Food for Thought www.foodforthought-chicago.com
- Photography: Artisan Events www.artisanevents.com
- Spa Services: Beauty On Call www.beautyoncall.com
- Cocktails: Airforce Nutrisodas www.nutrisoda.com

Toast to Leap Year, Page 40

- Caterer: Boutique Bites www.boutiquebites.com
- Photography: Carasco Photography www.carascophoto.com
- Rentals: Tablescapes www.tablescapes.com
- Linen: BBJ Linen www.bbjlinen.com
- Dessert: Julius Meinl www.juliusmeinl.com www.sugarfixe.com

An Oscar Dinner, Page 48

- Venue: Private home
- Caterer: Chef Art Smith www.chefartsmith.net
- Rentals: Classic Party Rentals www.classicpartyrentals.com
- Linens: Custom, Resource One www.resourceone.info
- Cake: Sam Godfrey, Perfect Endings
- Photography: George Burns, georgeburnsphotography.com

A Fabulous, French Affair, Page 56

- Venue: Private home
- Caterer: Food for Thought www.foodforthought-chicago.com
- Rentals: Tablescapes www.tablescapes.com
- Linens: BBJ Linen www.bbjlinen.com

Retirement Dinner, Page 62

- Venue and Caterer: Spiaggia Private Dining Room, Chef Tony Mantuano: www.levyrestaurants.com
- Photography: George Burns georgeburnsphotography.com
- Rentals: Tablescapes www.tablescapes.com

- Linens: BBJ Linen
  www.bbjlinen.com
- Cakes: Cakegirls
  www.thecakegirls.com

A Windy City 40th, Page 72
- Venue, Caterer and Linens: Boka, Chef Giuseppe Tentori
  www.bokachicago.com
- Photography: Artist Group
  www.artistgroup.net

Dinner in Paris, Page 80
- Linens: Windy City Linen
  www.windycitylinen.com
- Photography: Avery House
  www.averyhouse.net

A Taste of Tuscany, Page 88
- Venue and Caterer: Table 52, Chef Art Smith
  www.tablefifty-two.com
- Photographer: Jason Geil
  www.jasongeil.com
- Linens: BBJ Linen
  www.bbjlinen.com
- Cookies, Truffles: Take the Cake
  www.takethecakeetc.com
- Cake: Vanille Patisserie
  www.vanillepatisserie.com
- Cupcakes: Sugar Bliss
  www.sugarblisscakes.com

Birthday Times Two, Page 96
- Venue: River East Art Center
  www.rivereastartcenter.com
- Caterer: J&L Catering
  www.jandlcatering.com
- Photography: Amanda Hein
  www.amandahein.com
- Entertainment: The Ken Arlen Orchestra: www.arlenmusic.com
- Linens: Ruth Fischl, Inc.
  www.ruthfischl.com

A Cinderella Birthday, Page 106
- Venue: Private home
- Caterer: Food for Thought
  www.foodforthought-chicago.com
- Tent: Partytime Productions
  www.partytimeproductions.com
- Rentals: Tablescapes
  www.tablescapes.com
- Linens: BBJ Linen
  www.bbjlinen.com
- Cake: Vanille Patisserie
  www.vanillepatisserie.com

Gentlemen, Start Your Engines, Page 114
- Venue: Private home
- Caterer: Jewell Events Catering
  www.jewelleventscatering.com
- Photography: La Storia Foto
  www.lastoriafoto.net
- Rentals: Tablescapes
  www.tablescapes.com
- Linens: BBJ Linen
  www.bbjlinen.com

Girly Pedi Party, Page 122
- Venue: A Perfect Event
  www.aperfectevent.com
- Photography: Artisan Events
  www.artisanevents.com
- Linens: Ruth Fischl
  www.ruthfischl.com
- Spa Services: Beauty On Call
  www.beautyoncall.com

Hey Baby—Couples 'n Cocktails, Page 132
- Venue: Private Home
- Caterer: Winston's Market
  www.winstonsmarket.net
- Cake: Alliance Bakery
  www.alliance-bakery.com

Blue Willow Bridal Tea, Page 140
- Venue: Private Home
- Caterer: Jewell Events Catering
  www.jewelleventscatering.com
- Photography: Artist Group
  www.artistgroup.net
- Rentals: Tablescapes
  www.tablescapes.com
- Linens: Carousel Linen
  www.carousellinen.com

Spring's New Arrival, Page 146
- Venue: Private Home
- Caterer: Elegant Edge
  www.elegantedge.com
- Rentals: Tablescapes
  www.tablescapes.com
- Linens: BBJ Linen
  www.bbjlinen.com

Engagement Cocktails, Page 156
- Venue: Room 1520
  www.room1520.com
- Caterer: Entertaining Company
  www.entertainingcompany.com
- Rentals: Tablescapes
  www.tablescapes.com
- Photography: Avery House
  www.averyhouse.net
- Linens: Carousel Linen
  www.carousellinen.com

"I Do" Dinner, Page 162
- Venue: Inn at Palmetto Bluff
  www.palmettobluffresort.com
- Photography: Avery House
  www.averyhouse.net

Lilly Pulitzer Tea Party, Page 168
- Venue: Casa Palmero, Pebble Beach: www.pebblebeach.com
- Catering/Décor: Pebble Beach
- Linens: A Perfect Event
  www.aperfectevent.com
- Photography: Eric Lowe
- Photography: Amanda Hein
  www.amandahein.com

Cypress Sunset Soiree, Page 174

- Venue: Private Home, Pebble Beach: www.pebblebeach.com
- Caterer/Decor: Pebble Beach www.pebblebeach.com
- Photography: Davina + Daniel www.davina+daniel.com
- Linens: A Perfect Event www.aperfectevent.com

Dinner on the Lake, Page 180

- Venue: Promontory Point www.hydeparkhistory.org/parks.html
- Caterer: Carlyn Berghoff Catering www.carlynberghoffcatering.com
- Photography: Rosalind Weddings www.rosalindweddings.com
- Jazz: Brent Kimbrough brentkimbrough.com

Lovely in the Low Country, Page 188

- Venue: Inn at Palmetto Bluff www.palmettobluffresort.com
- Photography: Avery House www.averyhouse.net

Celebration in the City, Page 194

- Ceremony, Reception and Caterer: The Chicago Hilton and Towers www.chicagohilton.com
- Photography: La Storia Foto www.lastoriafoto.net
- Entertainment: The Ken Arlen Orchestra: www.arlenmusic.com
- Rentals: Tablescapes www.tablescapes.com
- Linens: BBJ Linen www.bbjlinen.com
- Wedding Cake Cookie Favors: Take the Cake www.takethecakeetc.com
- Eco-Friendly Cocktail: Vodka 360 www.vodka360.com

A Seaside Celebration, Page 202

- Venue: The Lodge and Beach Club, Pebble Beach www.pebblebeach.com
- Caterer/Decor: Pebble Beach www.pebblebeach.com
- Photography: Davina + Daniel www.davina+daniel.com

Antique Ambience, Page 208

- Ceremony: St. Michael's Church www.st-mikes.org
- Reception: Murphy Auditorium www.murphyauditorium.com
- Caterer: Carlyn Berghoff Catering www.carlynberghoffcatering.com
- Photography: Rosalind Weddings www.rosalindweddings.com
- Entertainment: The Dick Judson Orchestra www.dickjudsonorchestra.net
- Linens: Carousel Linen www.carousellinen.com
- Vintage Cake Toppers: Gold Bug Studio: www.goldbugstudio.com

Rustic Barn Romance, Page 216

- Ceremony: Private Home
- Reception: Private Barn
- Caterer: Blue Plate Catering www.blueplatechicago.com
- Photography: Artisan Events www.artisanevents.com
- Entertainment: Sue Conway Music www.billpollackmusic.com
- Linens: Custom, Carousel Linen www.carousellinen.com

A 110th Anniversary, Page 226

- Venue and Caterer: Madame Tartine: www.madametartine.com
- Photographer: Avery House www.averyhouse.net
- Linens: Carousel Linen www.carousellinen.com
- Cake and Cupcakes: Dinkel's Bakery, Sugar Bliss www.dinkelsbakery.com www.sugarbliss.com

A Toast to Friendship, Page 232

- Hanging Lanterns: Trillium, www.trilliumnantucket.com
- Lobster: East Coast Seafood, www.nantucketfoodandwine.com
- Nantucket Clam Chowder, www.theseagrille.com
- Wine: Nantucket Vineyard, ciscobrewers.com
- Beer: Cisco Brewery, ciscobrewers.com

A Perfect 10, Page 242

- Venue: A Perfect Event www.aperfectevent.com
- Caterer: Food for Thought www.foodforthought-chicago.com
- Caterer: Blue Plate Catering www.blueplatechicago.com
- Caterer: Live-Action Sushi Station: Kaze Sushi www.kazesushi.com
- Caterer: Authentic Chicago Hot Dog Vendor: Andreas Catering www.andreascateringonline.com
- Photography: Artisan Events www.artisanevents.com
- Entertainment: Fig Media www.figmediainc.com
- Tent: Partytime Productions www.partytimeproductions.com
- Linens: BBJ Linen www.bbjlinen.com